Awakening
YOUR DESTINY

BRIDGING MONEY,
INTUITION AND YOUR
LIFE'S PURPOSE

LORRIE FEBUS

BALBOA.
PRESS
A DIVISION OF HAY HOUSE

Balboa Press books may be ordered through booksellers or by contacting:

Balboa Press
A Division of Hay House
1663 Liberty Drive
Bloomington, IN 47403
www.balboapress.com
1-(877) 407-4847

Because of the dynamic nature of the Internet, any web addresses or links contained in this book may have changed since publication and may no longer be valid. The views expressed in this work are solely those of the author and do not necessarily reflect the views of the publisher, and the publisher hereby disclaims any responsibility for them.

ISBN: 978-1-4525-4479-3 (sc)
ISBN: 978-1-4525-4516-5 (e)

Library of Congress Control Number: 2012903504

The author of this book does not dispense medical advice or prescribe the use of any technique as a form of treatment for physical, emotional, or medical problems without the advice of a physician, either directly or indirectly. The intent of the author is only to offer information of a general nature to help you in your quest for emotional and spiritual well-being. In the event you use any of the information in this book for yourself, which is your constitutional right, the author and the publisher assume no responsibility for your actions.

Any people depicted in stock imagery provided by Thinkstock are models, and such images are being used for illustrative purposes only. Certain stock imagery © Thinkstock.

Printed in the United States of America

Balboa Press rev. date: 2/24/2012

About the Author

Lorrie Febus is a financial executive and consultant. After nearly 20 years in corporate America, climbing the proverbial ladder to success, she realized she was not living her dream. As a single mother, she took a leap of faith and left her safe, corporate career and embarked on a journey of discovery and passion.

She discovered using knowledge, focus, and intuition she could create a joy filled life. She used these tools to attract her husband, become a successful investor and business owner, and to create abundance in all areas of her life. She has discovered her lineage and the life of her dreams.

She is passionate about helping others improve their lives using these tools. She is a success and business coach and has coached for top trainers. She was called back to the corporate world during this current economic crisis to utilize her expertise in the financial industry and knowledge of the real estate market.

Lorrie's gift is bridging two worlds. Using her practical financial and business knowledge and intuitive energy to help her clients discover their authentic self to empower their future. She provides real life solutions to integrate with everyday living to create unlimited success through empowerment, knowledge, focus and intuition.

Using success and energy techniques she believes we can manifest everything we desire, joy and peace. By opening heart energy and allowing spirit to shine through, we can change our lives and the world.

Visit her website www.moneymindempower.com. You can sign up for free weekly tools, thoughts and techniques.

Dedication

To my husband Wayne Febus and my mother Lillian Omine. Thank you for always believing in me and my journey.

With Gratitude,
Lorrie

Contents

Introduction:
You Are an Adventurer!

Mary awakens to her blaring alarm clock. She hurriedly, moves through the dawn racing to her mediocre, unfulfilling job. She wishes she had the courage to leave. As she drives down the road in a familiar trance, the newscaster on the radio drones on about the deepening economic recession reporting an increase in unemployment numbers. As she listens to the news, her thoughts drift to her own job and how she will probably not receive a pay increase this year. She reaffirms silently how unfair this is. Her thoughts continue to drift to her over-obligated schedule, and her anxiety goes up another notch. Her day at work is spent in hyper drive wishing she were somewhere else. Needing the money to pay the bills, she pushes on. In the break room, she hears coworkers talk about the big game or the reality TV finale. They gossip about the lives of the movie stars, and real life drama. When the day is finished, she drives home on autopilot and mindlessly sings songs about broken hearts, taking jobs and shoving it, and partying until dawn. She remembers back when partying until dawn was fun and free. What happened to *that* girl? She cannot think of anything she does now for fun. What is fun anyway? Finally she returns home and decompresses on the sofa, spending the rest of the evening in a hypnotic state in front of the TV. She watches shows about desperate housewives, criminals, and tops it off with the late news covering a horrific account of the devastation of the most recent natural disaster. She drops in bed emotionally drained and without any energy left to move. She thinks about everything wrong with her job, her life and the world; how difficult life has been in the past and how worried she is about tomorrow.

This repeats day after day, and blends into weeks, months and years. As time goes by, her discontent increases. She knows there should be more to this life, but what and where to begin?

Now imagine yourself enjoying a relaxing walk on the beach. You can feel the sand between your toes, and delight in the cooling pleasure of the ocean as the waves draw upon the shore. Ahead of you, you notice a wooden box, dancing back and forth upon the shore in the tide. As you reach down curiously, you notice the uniqueness of this box. The etching feels vaguely familiar, like something in a dream from your childhood. You carefully open the box. Within the box, wrapped carefully in a plastic pouch, you find a book. This book is old, very old. As you carefully turn the fragile cover, the words on the page jump out at you.

You are more. The world awaits discovery of your gifts. It is time to Awaken Your Destiny.

This book you've discovered contains the answers to Mary's questions. It contains the answers to your own questions. Begin today, realizing you are destined for much more than the current life you are creating. Within these pages, dare to discover your unique gift to the world. Resound with joyful harmony in collaboration with the Universe.

This book is the book you imagined on that beach. This book is an adventure of discovery. You are the star of the show; a courageous superhero whose gifts, when discovered, will grace this world. You are the greatest adventurer in disguise. You have been disguised even from yourself until now. Learn to use your super power focus to discover your passion and strengths and follow synchronicities into the flow. Know that you have the tools to bridge current reality with the reality of your ideal destiny-fulfilled life. Have the courage of the superhero to go forward fearlessly.

Enjoy your adventure. Have fun with it. Most of all, don't take yourself too seriously. After all, who knows what you may discover during a relaxing walk on the beach!

Chapter 1:
The Adventure Begins

Imagine a place beyond the stars. This is a place where stars blanket the sky and shimmer like snowflakes on a moonlit night. It is peaceful, beautiful and serene. You are not in your physical body. You are a beautiful, luminescent spirit.

You are an eternal being of light—magnificent and unstoppable. You are pure positive energy—radiant and divine. You are the pure energy of joy, happiness and love. You have the ultimate power to manifest everything that you want.

In this world, you live with other luminescent spirits filled with love, joy and happiness. Life is sublime. One day, you learn about a new challenge and it intrigues you.

It is called Awaken Your Destiny on Earth.

This game is the rave of the Universe—the ultimate challenge and the ultimate reality TV show. It sounds like fun, and you are all about fun!

Good news!

You've passed the audition! Hooray, you have earned your game pass to Earth. You are an amazing being of light; able to transcend all fears and manifest all dreams- ready to enter the game. Hang on to your hat! Here you go.

Wait, hold on! Did anyone give you details on how to win the challenge?

No? You are in luck! It is never too late to start living deliberately. Now that you have this book things may become clearer.

Let's start with the basics. In this game, you live in a world of materialism (imagine that?) and face a myriad of obstacles.

This challenge is like nothing you have experienced before. First, it occurs on a strange planet called Earth. This planet Earth has mountains, oceans, land masses, sky and water. These elements were created just for you and other adventurers. The topography and everything on this planet is made up of material elements. Imagine that! The energy fields still exist, of course; however, they can't be viewed as obviously as the material elements. This planet has of all things a gravity field, which means you can no longer float or flitter about and get to places with just an idea or thoughts. Cool a gravity field!

The biggest challenge is once you arrive on Earth you forget who you truly are. You develop cosmic amnesia forgetting that you are a divine, magnificent, pure positive luminescent energy. Once on Earth, you believe that you are your physical body, and your material stuff is a reflection of who you are. HA! What a twist, a head game, a wild ride!

Before you depart Infinity, you select a team. Part of your team will be chosen for the adventure too. The other half of your team will remain in infinity, helping to guide you on your journey. You and the team members adventuring to Earth, plan before your departure, when you will meet up again on Earth to help each other closer to victory. The challenge is once in Earth's atmosphere, your team members who are accompanying you will not remember the essence of their magnificence either, and what or how they are supposed to help you. Once you arrive on Earth, you may no longer recognize each other in your human body disguises. Also, the help they provide to help you toward victory, may be perceived on the material plane as something undesirable. It will make it even more fun and challenging to achieve victory. Whoa, this is really a head game!

Your team members who remain in infinity help you by cheering you on and providing information to help you remember through a portal called your intuition. Here's the 'catch', many on Earth do not believe in intuition. They will likely discredit this form of communication, because it can't be measured or seen. You must learn to communicate with your infinite team in a material world. Additionally, your infinite team members cannot help you unless you ask for help. We have materialized these top secret messages only for your eyes, as postcards from Infinity.

✉ *Dear Multi-Dimensional Traveler,*

The sun rises and sets for you. The mountains, oceans, earth and sky were created just for you. You are a loving energy.
You are surrounded by other beautiful energies that make your heart sing.
You are and live in ultimate bliss and joy.
Remember this somewhere deep inside you when you travel to Earth.
Have FUN!

Infinity

To play this game, you are given a physical vehicle called a human body. Through this apparatus you can actually see, hear, smell, taste and touch the material elements on this planet.

You will learn to navigate your material terrain in this body. You arrive on Earth as a totally helpless being in this human body (small technicality). This human body is primitive, requiring daily care and maintenance. The better you care for your body, the longer you can experience the challenge and journey toward awakening your destiny. Once your body quits, your game is over. You will cease living on planet Earth. You will be rebirthed into the Infinite, and your spirit will remember its magnificence. The extreme victory is awakening your destiny and discovering your infinite magnificence while still in your human body so you may enjoy infinite freedom and the material sensations on Earth by bridging the two worlds. Yes, this is the challenge that has become the rave of the Universe!

At first, your survival is totally dependent on other magnificent energies trapped in human bodies who are already playing the game. These energies arrived on the earth plane before you, and have somewhat learned to survive the material terrain. They are playing the game with you and have also forgotten their greatness. You will learn about material life on Earth from these other humans. You will base most of what you will claim as reality from these first humans you contact, they are called your parents or family unit.

When you passed the audition, you became a Chosen One. You selected 2 cards. These cards are pre-selected before you travel to Earth. They are your Circumstances Card and your Destiny Card. Everyone on Earth has selected a unique set of cards. Once you arrive on Earth you have no option to change your cards.

Circumstances Card

You select a Circumstances Card prior to plopping into the game. This card determines where you will start your adventure. Some Earth scenarios are more challenging than others. You may have signed up for the easy play or hard play version. The scenario on the card determines the human family, your physical attributes (race, gender and socio-economic status), and location on Earth where you will begin playing the game. You may arrive into a family unit that is abusive, dysfunctional or uncaring. Some adventurers are raised without a family unit and learn to survive in even more challenging circumstances. No worries. When you selected your card, you chose your life scenario. You knew the level of challenge that you are capable of overcoming. When your journey of contrast is greater, your level of play and victory is even more celebrated. You are truly an adventurer!

Dear Winner,

Yes!! You made it! Know that I am your biggest, brightest, most adoring fan. You may have forgotten your greatness, but I remember.
Here's a hint: Your first step in this game is to appreciate your chosen circumstances. This may be where you start your game, but it will

not be where you end the game—especially now that you have this book.

Your Greatest Admirer,
Infinity

Your reality blueprint can shape your entire material outlook on Earth. Your blueprint is formed—usually unconsciously as a child—based on your circumstances. Your family unit or other key players will teach you to believe that you are the sum of your mind, intellect and body. They feel it is their duty to teach you what is right, responsible and required socially to be accepted in the society they have created. The longer you remain on Earth the more likely you are to move further from remembering your own greatness. Keep in mind, these other humans are also playing the game, and are still trying to navigate their way through the pitfalls of the game. The reality blueprint they share with you via their beliefs, actions and words may be a hindrance rather than help toward ultimately winning the game. Nevertheless, your divine, beautiful Self can create a new reality blueprint.

Destiny Card

The other card you select is your destiny card. Your destiny card reveals something you are destined to do, which positively impacts life on Earth. This is your mission to accomplish on Earth. Your goal is to discover and perform your pre-chosen destiny or mission in the game. You knew coming in that you would make Earth a better place. Everyone's destiny card is unique, and all destiny cards can be simultaneously achieved. This is huge! All destiny cards can be simultaneously achieved! All adventurers have the opportunity to win the challenge regardless of how many others win. We are not playing against others; we are playing *with* others, helping everyone get closer to their chosen destiny. The earth plane is abundant!

This game is the ultimate virtual reality challenge. It is also extremely interactive. What you do or don't do can change the entire outcome of your game, and maybe even the planet Earth. What you do will directly affect the lives of other adventurers.

 Insight:

How You Win the Challenge

You are victorious when you fulfill your Destiny, discover your passion or your unique gift to the world, reclaim your infinite magnificence and overcome your cosmic amnesia while still in your human body on Earth.

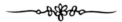

Okay, now what?

You're stuck on Earth with cosmic amnesia – what are you supposed to do now?

One of the main reasons you volunteered for this challenge– is to have fun!

☒ *Dear Fun Lover,*

I admire your courageous soul for playing this game. Just a reminder– you already know everything you need to know to awaken your destiny.

Your Greatest Admirer,
Infinity

Your Navigational System

You are given a multi- dimensional, invisible, intergalactic compass at the beginning of the challenge called your emotional navigational system. This tool, called emotions, is a measuring device, which indicates whether or not you are going in the direction of your destiny. Good feeling emotions transmit a higher frequency and bring you closer toward hearing your infinite team through intuition. Bad feeling emotions transmit a lower frequency, which keeps your bound to the materialism of Earth and blocks your connection to the universe. The bad feelings are useful as they provide you the contrast to want to improve your emotional feeling. This is the navigational system at work. Love and joy are the highest frequency emotions and can raise your energy field when you feel them. The higher your energy field vibrates, the closer you come to recognizing your greatness and utilizing your ability to manifest and create the life you want on Earth.

✉ *Dear Soul Seeker,*

You are in good hands. Keep your vibration high by feeling appreciation and love. The higher your vibration, the clearer your channel to us becomes.

In Ever Loving Frequency,
  Infinity

Remember the biggest commitment you make when you decide to play is you forget all of who you truly are. You agree to forget that you are a divine, magnificent, pure positive energy. One of your missions is to remember who you really are while on Earth.

Your Human Body

The challenge is over when your human body vehicle quits.

Instructions on the care and maintenance of your human body will come from the other earth travelers before you. Basically, this vehicle does not come with an instruction manual and all knowledge is learned through trial and error. This vehicle requires daily attention to keep it running optimally via food, water, and exercise. There is an optimal amount of each of these to keep your vehicle running at peak performance. This amount will vary between vehicles, depending on size, circumstances, location and other factors.

Initially, when you are a baby on Earth, you will depend on other earthlings to help you survive. As you get older, most instruction is on teaching you how to not hurt or damage your vehicle. Once your vehicle is permanently damaged it can impact your senses and how you relate to the material world. Your Earth challenge is over if your vehicle is damaged beyond the point of repair. On Earth they call this dying or death. In that flash of moment you will realize all the worry and fear were just an illusion. And what an illusion it was! All the time and energy spent worrying about money, relationships, acceptance, and not enough time – all an illusion, all the fear of not enough, and poverty – all an illusion. HA! What a wild ride!

⊠ *Dear Fun Lover,*

Know that when your time on Earth is over, you will remember everything – your greatness, your joy, your magnificence and most of all that Earth was just a game. Believe me, it all happens so fast. One minute you are on Earth, and the next you are back here in the cosmos – game over. And the minute your soul leaves your earthly body you will discover that what you thought was real simply wasn't. In uproarious laughter you will realize it was just for fun and you will say, I want to play again!!

Waiting to join you in Laughter,
  Infinity

Those are the basic instructions. Ready to play?

I am cheering you on, and look forward to you awakening your destiny.

The basic details for the Awaken Your Destiny adventure are as follows:

1. You have cosmic amnesia and have forgotten you are a magnificent Being comprised of pure, powerful energy. You will spend time

(an exclusive earthly concept) maintaining an earthly reality. This reality is largely based on material objects and objectives. Your challenge is to acknowledge and reclaim your greatness. You will need to learn to manifest material objects (another earthly concept). Reclaiming your joy and bliss on the earthly plane and enjoying the journey – this is what it is all about!

2. To play the game you are given a vehicle or a physical apparatus called a body. This vehicle requires care and maintenance. The better you care for your vehicle, the longer you can experience the game on Earth. Once your vehicle quits, your game is over. The extreme victory is winning the game while still having your vehicle running well to enjoy all sensations on Earth. This is why you signed up to play in the first place!

3. You pick your Circumstances Card when you decide to play. Whatever card you are dealt is where you will start your game. You pre-selected the human family, physical and material attributes (race, gender and socio-economic status), and location on Earth when you decided to play the game. Some scenarios are more challenging than others – you may have signed up for the easy or hard version of the game. You make it what it is.

4. Your reality is what you are creating, with every thought, word and emotion.

5. When you elect to play the game, you also select a Destiny Card, which positively impacts life on Earth. This Destiny Card is your mission to accomplish while playing the game on Earth. These cards are geared toward helping others playing the Earth game or other living creatures on earth (including the planet itself).

6. You are also given tools to help you navigate through the game and toward success. One of the tools you are given at the beginning of the game is a navigational system called your emotions. Love and joy are the highest frequency emotions and can raise your energy vibration when you feel them. The higher your energy field can vibrate the closer you become to recognizing your greatness, awakening your destiny, and utilizing your ability to manifest and create what you want in your life.

You win when you accomplish two things:

1. Share your unique gift with the world, therefore fulfilling your pre chosen Destiny Card.
2. Reclaim your power as a magnificent, beautiful energy here on the earth plane, and create the joy-filled life of your dreams.

Setting the Stage

Congratulations! Now that you know how powerful you are, let's have some fun!

Here we go!

Plop! You land right where you are Today. You are in the circumstances you pre-selected upon playing the game.

Beginning now, at whatever your chronological earth age, it is the perfect age for you to begin discovering you are a superhero.

Imagine, you are playing the ultimate reality game show.

In a popular reality TV show, players are dropped off on a remote location, usually on an island in the middle of the ocean, with a cast of characters, setting out to discover their new surroundings. Each player is setting out to win the treasure prize of the game, which will bring them material happiness.

Similarly, you are 'dropped off' on the planet Earth in the middle of the universe.

Uniquely, the playing field here is multi-dimensional.

At a glance, the earth world appears to be based on materialism. Your earth vehicle or body comes equipped with material senses to traverse this terrain. The senses of sight, sound, hearing, feeling, and taste give the ability to exist in this material world and preserve your primitive, fragile body. You are able to sense danger or something life threatening to your vehicle body with these senses. These senses also enable you to navigate and enjoy your earth terrain. Throughout your adventure here on Earth you will encounter different characters. All of them are great, magnificent energies with cosmic amnesia, and all trying to accomplish their destiny to win their challenge – although they may not know it yet. These characters will be in various stages of 'spiritual or cosmic remembering' development.

Rediscovering their own great, magnificent spirit, and overcoming their cosmic amnesia. Most of these encounters will have a message for you. The good news is, unlike some reality shows, all players can win this game simultaneously! You are meant to help each other toward your personal discovery. Everyone can be a winner!

Although you were dropped here, you are never alone. Imagine the loving energy of the Universe surrounding you – like the air you breathe, silent and unseen. The Universe would not have dropped you here in the middle of space, on Earth, all on your own. Especially since you have cosmic amnesia, forgetting you are created from magnificent Source Energy.

There is an audience, much like the TV audience, who cheer and root for your success. They are your raving fans! This is the part of your team that stayed in Infinity. They want to give advice to their favorite player – You. You will be able to hear their guidance, if you listen carefully through your intuition. Amongst these magnificent beings are your Angels, Spirit Guides and Ancestors. You may not be able to see them, but they can see you. They revel in the glory of your triumphs and send you guidance during times of earthly existence. They are always cheering for you and if you listen in times of quiet during your day- you may hear them!

✉ *Dear Fun Sparkling One,*

Ha!! Do you remember yet? This is you!! You are our hero.
We are having a great time cheering for you and watching your every move. We know you can do it! You can win! We will be with you every step of the way.
Next time around, I want to play and you can cheer for me!

Your Friend,
* Infinity*

Further imagine and superimpose your current life being lived in the context of this adventure being plopped on a reality TV island called Earth. You grow up learning how to traverse our material terrain through each of your senses. You discover what you physically like and don't like in the material world, and how to keep your human vehicle from getting injured. Each person creates a task oriented life and relationships with the others based on their senses and emotions. Most follow a linear path and do what is expected of them. They go to school, have a job or career, get married, and have a family. At times you may question the path, and wonder if this is all there is to life. In quiet times your consciousness (your infinite audience) whispers, there *IS* more to life. At first you ignore this voice, not having the courage to acknowledge the words. The louder this voice gets, the harder it becomes to ignore. At first you keep yourself very busy, to avoid having any quiet time in which the voice may arise. Then 'busy' becomes 'stressed', and this no longer works- the hole of discontent is growing. To fill this void we often seek power, fame or money hoping to gain enough of these things to fill the void. We may go for a quick fix to satisfy the void with shopping, food, alcohol, or another physical pleasure. This works for a while, but then the need grows and it takes more and more substance as the addiction and discontent grows. The fix activity actually begins to feed the discontent. Deep down you are afraid you have really lost your way. You continue to go through the motions of life. You feel stuck, and time goes by.

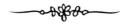

 Insight:

Addiction fills the void of not being in alignment or on the path of your Destiny

People spend a lifetime searching for happiness; looking for peace. They chase idle dreams, addictions, religions, even other people, hoping to fill the emptiness that plagues them. The irony is the only place they ever needed to search was within.
– Romana L. Anderson

Remember the challenge? Most players are busy doing their daily jobs within their reality and, with their cosmic amnesia, have forgotten the challenge. You come into this reality with no memory of your true magnificence. You may have forgotten your true nature of joy, radiance and positive energy. You may have forgotten you have a universal crowd cheering you on, and guiding your way to fulfillment through sharing your unique gift. It is your time to start remembering!

 Insight:

Aware or not, you are participating in the Awakening Your Destiny adventure. Embrace this challenge and live deliberately.

Life is an adventure, dare it.
– Mother Theresa

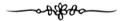

Have the courage to believe you are an undiscovered superhero – a mild mannered Clark Kent who does not know he is really Superman! You have a destiny to fulfill.

Have the courage to say, "Yes, all change is possible!"

Remember, everyone can win the Awaken Your Destiny challenge. All it takes is a courageous spirit willing to have faith in the Universe.

From this point forward commit. Commit yourself with every fiber of your being to reveal the superhero you are deep inside. Like a skydiver who leaps from the plane, at the moment she jumps, she is committed to the experience. Like the bungee jumper, at the moment he leaps off the bridge, he is committed to the experience. Like Luke Skywalker in the movie Star Wars, once he accepts becoming a Jedi, he is committed to accepting this power and knowledge. He is committed, and his life will never be the same. He is a Jedi. No turning back. There is no middle ground. Do you accept now, and commit to discovering your destiny? It is a state of being, a consciousness you are committing to accept. Clarity of knowledge and power will be bestowed upon you, as your training progresses. If yes, light a ceremonial candle, state your acceptance, commitment to the Universe and proceed.

 Dear Great One,

We are filled with glee to see you have accepted discovering your divine destiny! We are committed with you. Do you hear us yet? Can you see us yet? We are giddy in anticipation of being graced by your presence again. It may seem difficult at times- know we are here ready to do anything you ask. Your words are more powerful than you know!

Your Humble Servant,
   Infinity

Chapter 2:
The Power of Words,
Thoughts and Beliefs

This is when the real fun begins. Let's begin tangibly by making some conscious choices on a daily basis to redirect your life toward overcoming your cosmic amnesia, and creating the joy filled life of your dreams.

Before you left Infinity, you picked your Circumstances Card. Your family, race, national origin, socio-economic status, genetic pre-disposition etc., any circumstance you were born into was pre-selected by your infinite self. The more challenging your circumstance – the more you knew you had the power to overcome! Ahhh – such is the magnificence of all knowing!

All other elements of your current physical reality is created by you-through your words, thoughts and beliefs. This means you created every circumstance currently in your life.

This means since you create your life, you are no longer a victim. You are a creator. No longer can anyone do any thing to you that makes you a victim. Victim mentality, or blaming others for things gone wrong in your life is denying that you are a great creator! Take responsibility for everything in your life. Your reality on Earth is what you are creating with every thought and word. You may not have been consciously creating unwanted things in your life, but nonetheless, you created them – consciously or unconsciously, positively or negatively.

This is good news! You are no longer a victim of any circumstance - past, present or future. You are liberated! You are a creator!

The first challenge in the game is you must master your words, thoughts and beliefs to advance to the next level of play.

Words and Thoughts

Your words are a powerful tool of creation. What you say, and how you say it, matters. On the surface, you may think your words are merely a way to communicate with others. This may be true in a linear world. For example, you speak words, someone else hears your words, and interprets your thought and comprehends what you are saying. This is basic communication; something we do every day. Now let's think multi-dimensionally. You speak words; the Universe hears your words, interprets your thought and *creates* what you are saying. Yes, creates what you are saying. Words are not only for communication. Every word you speak is a seed of creation.

Here's the twist, the seed is planted, whether you want it in your life or not. You may talk about being poor in your childhood. The seed that is planted is poor. This is what you are cultivating in your life. If you say, life is hard. The seed that is planted is having a hard life. If you say, My life is going nowhere. The seed you plant is a stagnant life. The more you talk about your woes, the deeper you etch the ruts in your path. These words are creating this belief system into your reality.

Words and thoughts= Energy

We live in a world of energy. Everything around us is energy. Every living thing, every material object, every word spoken and every thought we have are all energy. Words and thoughts are the energy in the creation of material manifestation. Using positive words and thoughts are a key to moving this energy forward. Using words carelessly, jokingly, or negatively can result unknowingly in creating an undesirable situation.

In addition, making yourself less than or smaller in the guise of humility can be very detrimental. Accepting a complement graciously is a powerful action. When someone gives you a complement the powerful response is, "Thank you".

 Insight:

It is imperative that your thoughts, words and feelings are in alignment with desires.

Life consists of what a man is thinking of all day.
  – Ralph Waldo Emerson

Here are basic lessons the use of words and thoughts.
- Always state your words in a positive manner.
- Be very clear on your intention. Think before you speak.
- Take every word and thought literally, the Universe doesn't know sarcasm or joking.
- Be certain the words you say are congruent with your thoughts and feelings.

✉ *Hello My Great One,*

Just a friendly reminder. I cannot read your mind. I cannot determine which things you really want, and what you don't want, due to a missing frequency transmission from the planet Earth.
All your thoughts become things. Think and speak carefully!

Over and Out,
  Infinity

You think your thoughts and the Universe interprets your thought and creates what you are thinking. Thoughts and words are not only for communication. They are tools of creation. Every thought you think and word you speak is a seed of creation.

When you think something, whether you say it verbally or not, you begin the creation process.

 Insight:

Create consciously.
When you think of something you want, you attract it.
When you think of something you don't want, you attract it.

Remember that your mind guides you toward the thing you think about most. Spend no time, therefore, in thinking of the things you DO NOT WANT, for this is precisely the same as hoping and wishing for the things you don not want.
– Napoleon Hill

Beliefs

Beliefs are thought and word patterns that have been ingrained into your core self. These are thoughts, which at some time in your life you internalized, consciously or subconsciously and made them a truth for you in your world. Your beliefs become a defining limitation, whether your belief is the world is flat, you are not smart enough, you will always be poor because making money is hard, or you are not good enough in some way or another. It is required for each mighty adventurer is to break out of limiting belief patterns, to limitless belief patterns. After all, if you are to overcome the cosmic amnesia, you need to believe you are limitless. There are no limits for you in this physical world!

✉ *Dear Adventurer,*

You are AMAZING! You are figuring it out. Just like a big multi-dimensional puzzle. We wish we could have told you earlier about

the word and thought thing. We know you can live outside the box.
We love living vicariously through you on your adventure on Earth.

Infinity

Using a plant analogy, how do plants miraculously grow? Basically, you have some soil, you plant a seed in the soil, give it appropriate energy- water, sunshine, fertilizer; and it will grow into a living flourishing plant. Creation is the same formula. To create something in your life you plant a seed, add the appropriate energy, and it will grow into a material manifestation. You have been using this formula for everything you have created in your life thus far, whether you know it or not. Let's break down the elements of creation.

Seed = Words and Thoughts

Soil = Beliefs

Energy = all things in the Universe

The soil or your belief is where you plant your seed. Your beliefs give your seed the signal to grow. Have you ever planted a seed in the soil, and it did not grow? It seems the elements were there, but the seed did not sprout. Perhaps the soil was not suited for that type of seed. The seed, soil and energy were not in alignment for the plant to grow at this moment in time. It may sprout next season, as long as all elements are in alignment.

It is the same for words and thoughts. If your words, thoughts and beliefs are not in alignment your seed will not grow at this moment in time. It may sprout in the future, once all the elements are in alignment. You may have a backlog of seeds waiting to grow!

Your current beliefs will determine whether the seed (word or thought) you plant will grow at this moment in time.

You will not grow the seed of wealth if your underlying belief is you are poor.

You will not grow the seed of passive wealth if your underlying belief is that you must work hard for your money.

You will not grow the seed of a harmonious marriage if your underlying belief is partners often disagree.

You will not grow the seed of abundance if your underlying belief is one of lack.

You will not grow the seed of perfect health if your belief is you come from unhealthy genetics.

Dear Eternal Gardner,

You have the greenest thumb we have ever seen! You are sowing and growing every seed you plant. You are even growing the seeds you didn't want to plant. Please be careful and choose every seed wisely. Your flourishing garden depends on it.

Enjoying Your Beauty,
  Infinity

Your belief system is the soil into which you are planting all your seeds. You want to cultivate and nourish your soil to be in alignment with the seeds you wish to blossom in your life.

It is worth noting, if your subconscious belief is one of poor, and your words and thoughts plant seeds of poor – poverty will be created in your life. The Universe does not know whether the thoughts, words and beliefs you have in your alignment are truly what you want in your life. When all the elements are in alignment, you manifest, or grow, whatever it is you have planted. You may be creating the life you don't want by not knowing this powerful tool.

🦋 **Insight:**

Use your words, thoughts and beliefs to create what you want in your life.

Plant the seed of desire in your mind and it forms a nucleus with power to attract to itself everything for its fulfillment.
– Robert Collier

The first step is to be aware of your words and thoughts. Only use words and think thoughts of what you desire in your life. Consciously refocus your thought, if you slip and an undesirable thought or words creep in. Stop the undesirable thought, and replace it with a desired outcome. Stop using non-empowering words like can't, but, or try. Remember in the movie Star Wars when Yoda tells Luke, Do or Do not – there is no try. Only talk about what you want to draw into your life. No more gossiping. No more grumbling about people, places or things in your life. No more talking about bad situations in the past. No talking about calamities, which may happen in the future. No more talking about how you have been wronged by someone or something in an attempt to make you feel better by gaining the sympathy of others. No more griping about the weather, your parents, your ex-husband, or teenaged kids. No more talking about other people's bad situations to make your own situation seem better.

These may be big changes for you. Big or small, these changes are required for you to blossom into the superhero you are inside. Talk about what you are creating. Talk about a project you are excited about. Talk about fun things. Talk about extraordinary things people have done. Talk about things that inspire you. Talk about good things. Talk about your abundance. Talk about how lucky you are. Better yet, talk about and feel lucky and abundant.

✉ Dear TV Commentator,

We do not want to hear the blow by blow of every situation occurring around you. It is all OLD news! Ha! That stuff was created millennia ago. We want to hear words about the fresh things you are creating NOW. Everything you want in your life, the excitement of the journey ahead, and all your dreams of grandeur. Just because it isn't materializing yet doesn't mean it is not happening. Now you are talking!

Awaiting Your Breaking News Updates,
　　Infinity

The next step is cultivating a receptive belief system for manifesting what you desire.

The challenge is many of our beliefs are so deeply ingrained in our psyche we may not even know they exist. More than likely, you learned many of these beliefs consciously or unconsciously from your earth pod or family unit. This is where we begin our discovery of our beliefs.

There are 5 main areas where we may hold a limiting belief system.

- Self (worthiness or self-esteem)
- Relationships
- Money
- Physical body
- Spiritual

We all have underlying beliefs in each of these areas. Some beliefs we hold are empowering and others are limiting. Not all beliefs are limiting. They are only limiting when they are manifesting or creating undesired situations in your life.

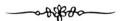

 Insight:

Let go of your limiting beliefs.
By changing your beliefs, you can change your life.

The greatest revelation of our generation is the discovery that human beings, by changing the inner attitudes of their minds, can change the outer aspects of their lives.
  – William James

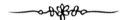

When our thoughts and beliefs align, the seeds we plant can sprout. Emotion is the catalyst which helps these seeds sprout quickly or slowly, or seemingly not at all.

Like with words, consciously or unconsciously, the positive or negative feeling or emotion about what you desire to create must be in alignment.

$\boxtimes$ *Dear Powerful One,*

Most humans think thoughts are uncontrollable things that have no affect until acted upon. HA! Wrong!

In Your Majesty,
  Infinity

Tools to reprogram your belief system

- Write and rewrite your new belief system over and over until it feels true for you.
- Say and use positive affirmations repetitively each day affirming your aligned belief.

- Create a visual vision board or book to view daily. Creating a collage of pictures and statements of what you desire in your life can help to affirm your belief system. Visually seeing your collaboration of images is very powerful. Place this board somewhere that you can see it daily. When viewing your images feel the emotion of living the images now in your imagination. Imagine with your all your senses.
- Surround yourself with other like-minded people, who have similar desires and beliefs.
- Visualizing with feeling is perhaps the most powerful method of aligning the energy of creation. When you are visualizing, the brain cannot tell the difference between a real or perceived event. Visualizing with feeling amplifies the vibration of the attraction. Each morning and evening while relaxing visualize your ideal life, and feel it with all your senses.

Chapter 3:
Beautiful Emotions

Emotions are a catalyst, when in alignment with what you want to manifest, can accelerate the process. Emotions are also an amazing tool given to you to help you navigate the earth terrain. Emotions are the navigational system that we secretly packed on board to help us on this adventure. Who knew? It is this guidance device that created the yearning for more and resulting emotional discontent. This guidance device or tool can help in determining whether you are on the right path on your adventure through your feelings. You will be able to accomplish your destiny with the masterful use of this tool.

Let's learn to use this fine, delicate instrument.
Perception is one of the key elements of this system.

Imagine you are at an amusement park, and have just strapped yourself into the biggest, scariest roller coaster, mostly due to your friends beckoning. Just as your car careens over the first big drop, and your stomach feels like it is in the middle of your throat you scream, "Stop the ride – I want to get off!" Well, of course the ride continues on – whether you want it to stop or not. You are fearful and worried. What if you get sick before the ride is over? What if you get derailed? What if you fly out of the car? You then scream out again, "Stop the ride!"

Now, consider this scenario:

You are at the same amusement park, and just as your car careens over the first big drop, and your stomach feels like it is in the middle of your throat you think, "Wow this is different. I can feel my adrenaline pumping. This feeling is something new, I don't know if I like it, but it feels like a new adventure. I know I am safe because the universe loves me. I am sure this experience exists only to bring me pleasure and joy. I will fully experience and choose to enjoy this ride! Whoa- ho!"

What does your life feel like?

Do you feel your life is like an out of control roller coaster ride and you want to scream, "Stop the ride! I want to get off!"

Or do you feel your life is an adventure every day, and brings you joy, fulfillment and happiness?

Either answer you choose, you are right.

🦋 Insight:

Your perception and positive feeling of the situation is far more important than the physical situation itself.

An optimist sees an opportunity in every calamity; a pessimist sees a calamity in every opportunity.
 – Winston Churchill

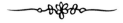

The physical situation of the roller coaster ride did not change, just the emotional perception of this ride. It is the perception of the situation, which evokes the emotion, not the actual situation. Your perception determines whether you will feel joy or fear.

Thus, perception, your attitude and thoughts can control your emotions.

Imagine you are walking into a dark room. You cannot see where you are going. All you have is a flashlight. You don't know anything about what is around you, only what you shine your light on. There are other people in this room with you, each with their own flashlight. Where ever they shine their light, or focus, creates their perception of the situation and the room. We could each be in the same space, focus our light on different objects and have a different perception of the room. What we take from each experience is relative to what we shine our light on.

A cosmic flashlight highlights your experience of events in your life. Your perception of an event is reflected in your feelings and emotion.

A positive perception results in good feelings.

A negative perception results in bad feelings.

Have you ever wondered why 2 people could go through the same experience and each may recall a very different scenario and perspective? Their cosmic flashlights were shining in different directions. This is similar to why siblings raised in the same household can have 2 very different views on life. Each day, each experience, it's all about perception. You can choose in each situation to shine your light on a positive or negative perspective or feeling. You can choose to focus in a good feeling emotion or a bad feeling emotion. Focusing on the positive, large or small, in every situation is your universal key to creation.

This test of perception is one of the greatest challenges in the material world. Allowing your cosmic flashlight to rule your emotions is reactive living. Consciously choosing positive perception and emotion regardless of what your cosmic flashlight reveals opens the doorway to manifesting your dreams.

Simply reacting to what life hands you, in events, emotion, feelings and thought, will create an endless cycle of reactive living.

The art of creation requires you to break out of this reactive living cycle. To break out of this cycle you must take focus off negative perception, and choose to focus on positive perception. This could be taking your focus off your current circumstances, which are not pleasing, and focusing good feelings forward into the life you are creating. Your emotions, feelings and thoughts should be focused on what you want in your life. This is where you want to shine your cosmic flashlight.

 Insight:

Reactive living to your material situation is perhaps the biggest pitfall of the game.

Your living is determined not so much by what life brings to you as by the attitude you bring to life; not so much by what happens to you as by the way your mind looks at what happens.
– John Homer Miller

Bob is a 'regular' guy, whose job was to clean out portable bathrooms. Each day he vacuums the sewage and sludge with a huge hose, sometimes getting some on himself. The stench is bad. After removing all the sewage, he wipes down the surfaces and floor. A pretty bad job by most peoples' standards, however, he is happy, positive and strives to do a good job. He wants to do the best job he can, and decides to have fun doing it. His circumstance does not control his emotion. His intention and thoughts control his emotion and perception. He is grateful to have a job, and grateful to be able to support his family. He knows he will not be doing this forever. As you probably already guessed, he is no longer cleaning potties. He created a new reality with his thoughts, attitude, and emotions.

When a circumstance makes you feel good, you want more of it, and should keep going in that direction. The bonus is when you can feel happy and joyful, in gratitude and abundance regardless of your circumstance; then you have mastered your material world. In addition, since like attracts like energetically, when you feel happy about the people, objects and experiences that vibrate joy in your life – you will attract more of these reasons to feel joyous. It is a positive creation loop.

This guidance system can also work in reverse and your emotions can create a negative emotional loop.

John is a 'cup half empty' kind of guy. He believes the world is out to get him. His office job is good by most peoples' standards. He is often annoyed at his customers, boss, co-workers and feels they are all incompetent at their jobs. He takes long breaks and checks out the sports stats on his computer daily. Each day, he trudges into the office, does his work, and goes home. He is a prisoner of his circumstance, having a bad day when things do not go his way. Most evenings he spends decompressing in front of the TV or playing mindless video games. John was recently laid off, with no current job prospects. He believes it is the story of his life - that he is just unlucky. This is a negative creation loop.

Dear Cosmic Navigator,

HA! Have you got it yet? Have you figured out how to use your navigational system? I wish I could have told you earlier. If I told you how simple it is you may not have believed me anyway.

In Emotional Splendor,
Your Infinite Crew

Creating Your Emotional State

Creating your emotional state based on positive perception and thought, despite your physical circumstances is the foundation of your ability to manifest in the physical world. Feeling positive emotion raises your vibration to the frequency of manifesting through thought. Manifesting in the material world is a key component to discovering your true power.

 Insight:

Positive feeling and having fun is a key component to manifesting in the material world.

Nothing can stop the man with the right mental attitude from achieving his goal; nothing on earth can help the man with the wrong mental attitude.
– W.W. Ziege

Unknowing adventurers let negative perceptions of their physical circumstances dictate their emotions. This is a tricky trap, which keeps you from discovering your power to create. Letting circumstances dictate your perception creates a negative loop, which dis-empowers you and makes you feel your situation is uncontrollable. It makes you feel as if your future is dependent on random luck to bring good circumstances for positive perception. In an attempt to feel better, some try to control their physical circumstances, to force good result. This requires hard work and vigilance, which can create stress by attempting to control every physical circumstance in your life. In this view- hard work and planning attempts to create good circumstances, to bring positive perception and emotions.

 Dear Clever One,

A tricky booby trap – what fun! You can dodge that bullet – just perceive the positive side of every situation. You know, look for that silver lining in the clouds. Wow, all that silver is positively magnetic!

Adoring Your Polarity,
Infinity

In a linear world concept:
Controlling physical circumstance hopefully creates favorable circumstance.

This brings occasional positive emotion. However, the requirement of control and the stress such control causes can become a constant negative energy drain, which eventually leads to a lower vibration. This can create a feeling of unhappiness and yearning for more.

Good news! The feeling of unhappiness or yearning for more is your navigational system at work! This feeling creates the drive to seek something more to fulfill your desire for happiness. This journey can lead to awakening your destiny – if you recognize the signs and have the proper tools!

Unfortunately, if you don't have the proper tools this cycle of feeling unfulfilled can lead you to seeking fulfillment through physical satisfaction. This can lead to addictions and obsession, which require more and more physical stuff or control to feel good. It can lead to a continual negative emotion cycle, which will take you down to lower and lower emotions from frustration, to anger, to hate, to rage and to depression. The linear world deals with depression by medicating to fill the void and repress the negative emotion. This is like purposely disconnecting the navigation system of an airplane in the middle of a flight. The airplane will likely never arrive at the intended destination, and will probably crash as a result.

 Dear Adventurer

Keep on feeling, keep on feeling – remember your destination and all the FUN you have at your fingertips! You are such a kidder- I know you remember that, right?

Infinity

Depression is simply your navigational system's signal you are off course. Suicide, or purposely aborting the mission, may cross the thought of an adventurer so lost they feel they cannot find their way home by accomplishing their destiny. Beautiful superheroes have temporarily lost their way because they do not have the proper information on how to utilize their navigational system. Lower range emotions simply indicate it is time to turn around and go the other way. Feel the emotion, and change your perception until you feel better. Keep going in the direction of better feeling thoughts, words, beliefs and perception.

There are 3 features of your emotional navigational system: range, consistency and intensity.

Range

The emotions we feel such as depression, anger and frustration are on the low range while happiness, joy and love are on the high range. Generally, high range feelings mean you are going toward your connection with the Universe, and low range feelings indicate you are going away from your connection with the universe. Lower range emotions are not bad and should not be suppressed or covered up. They are just your internal GPS system saying you are headed in the wrong direction. They serve as a warning that you are headed away from achieving your passion.

 Insight:

Being on the path toward your Destiny feels like happiness and fulfillment.

The happiness of your life depends upon the quality of your thoughts.
– Marcus Aurelius

In addition to accomplishing your destiny, the reason you chose to play is the element of the beauty of contrast. Your journey through the contrast of the physical world is what creates the wild ride. This element of contrast is powerful and will get your adrenaline pumping.

It is also a useful tool to help in determining the direction of your passion, and destiny in life.

It is important not to stuff down the bad emotions just because they feel bad.

Emotions in themselves are the gift of the material world. Knowing what you don't want in life, will lead you to what you do want. There are some things you may want in life that someone else may not care about at all. Emotions and feeling them, good or bad are a part of your unique navigational system. Feeling the full range of this gift of beautiful emotion is a universal blast! It doesn't matter what the emotion is, the key is for you to feel the emotion. Feel the emotion, and acknowledge it. When you get angry, acknowledge it and say, "Wow, I am so angry" and notice the feeling. Acknowledge what has created the angry feeling. Once you accept the anger you can move away from it, using your navigational system. From there, focus on the positive, in any situation and guide yourself toward the better more positive feeling. Any positive thought will do, as small as it may be. As you can work your way one thought at a time toward a better feeling, you increase your vibration and connection to intuition. Once you invoke your intuition, you are back in the game!

 *Dear Adventurer*

Okay, I know what you are thinking. Get real! Some things really make me angry. Good. Good. Good. There is not an emotion out there that is 'bad'. You came to the adventure to feel these wonderful emotions. How do the bad ones feel? How are they different from the good ones?
I can't wait until it is my turn to try!!

Adoring You from Afar,
  Infinity

Consistency

Keep your attention on how you feel. Focus on finding the better thought and the better feeling more often and for longer periods of time. Joy is a state of being. Joy can exist within us independent of whether things go our way or not. Only you can choose to allow a situation, person, or thing affect your state. In other words, you can choose to find the better feeling in every situation. Shine your light on the experiences you are magnetizing to you, and get excited about them. Feel the fun these experiences will bring and notice the higher range emotions of love, joy, passion, happiness, satisfaction, appreciation and fulfillment. Create more thoughts, which bring more of these feelings in your life. The more frequently you feel these emotions, the more good feelings you will attract.

The more often you can remain in the glowing vibration of love, joy and appreciation, the closer to your real cosmic self you are, and the more powerfully you will be able to regain your clarity of purpose and create what you want in this material world.

 Insight:

We make our reality.

The appearance of things change according to the emotions and thus we see magic and beauty in them, while the magic and beauty are really in ourselves.
　– Kahlil Gibran

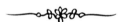

Within your true nature of good feelings and emotions is a magnificent power to create and manifest all your material desires. This magnificent power releases you from the circumstances of your existence to create the life of your dreams. Now that you are aware of your powerful emotional navigational system, you can choose your emotional state and consciously create your destination.

 Dear Adventurer,

The more you are living your life in the higher vibration frequencies of love and joy the clearer your connection to us. These better feeling

emotions eliminate the static from our lines. You can hear us give you direction, and cheats to help you win the game.

Keeping You Coming in Loud and Clear,
 Infinity

Intensity

Another distinct feature of your emotional navigational system is intensity. The more intense the emotion, either good or bad the more you amplify the magnetism and energy of your creation.

Intensity is like the gas pedal of your navigational system.

Intensity of the emotion increases your magnetism to bring the object of your thoughts to you faster in time. Whether these material manifestations are positive or negative, the more intense the emotions surrounding them, the quicker and more magnified the results will come to you.

 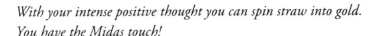

Dear Alchemist,

With your intense positive thought you can spin straw into gold. You have the Midas touch!

In Awe of Your Greatness,
 Infinity

In a multi-dimensional world concept:

Positive thought or perception regardless of circumstance = positive emotion = higher vibration.

This creates ability to manifest, which enables you to rise above the material world and awaken your destiny and reveal your passion bringing you fulfillment and enlightenment.

Insight:

What you focus on expands. Focus on the positive and it will expand. Focus on the negative and it will expand. You choose your focus each day, each situation, each moment.

No pessimist ever discovered the secret of the stars, or sailed to an uncharted land, or opened a new doorway to the human spirit.
– Helen Keller

Once you focus on creating positive perception and not positive circumstances, you will find you are on your way with your navigational system. Your navigational system will guide you via positive and negative feelings, toward the fun life your magnificent spirit intends to experience in the physical world. Learn to align your positive emotional energy before taking any action and you will able to create any material circumstance. As your flashlight of perception continues to shine joyfully on the positive, regardless of the situation, you will walk the path of your destiny and everything you want in life.

Chapter 4:
A World of Energy

Upon this earth terrain, there are laws of existence that are seen and unseen, which makes this game multi-dimensional. Everything on Earth is energy. Everything that sustains our human vehicle, from the food we eat, to the air we breathe is energy. The sounds we hear are energy. The light we see is energy. Our thoughts, words and beliefs are energy. They can either hold us in place or create a new reality. Something you cannot tangibly quantify, like your thoughts, can create material, physical things. What a twist! Now the FUN really begins!

 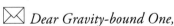

 Dear Gravity-bound One,

Earth must be like a fun house at the carnival! What an illusion that some on Earth do not believe in the energy of the universe. Ha, ha! Don't they know that energy is all there is? Jokesters! Energy is all there is!

Laughing Hysterically,
   Infinity

The world all around us is filled with energy. It is in and within everything we do. The energy manifests in physical and non-physical ways. Think of energy as an eternal life cycle of birthing and dying. Energy in its new fresh state is thoughts, ideas and inspiration- this is the planting or gestation cycle. Once it manifests into the material it is a birthing energy moving through the circle of life toward maturity and the dying process. Once and object is birthed and moving toward maturity, it is moving toward deterioration in the physical world. Once the physical object ceases to exist in the physical through death, it is re-birthed into pure energy and the cycle of begins again. Leaving material or physical form, does not mean the energy or spirit has died, it has been transformed or re-birthed into the infinite. Energy renews itself and this is the great cycle of the universe.

Change is good, as it brings fresh energy into a situation. Ones reaction to change, or emotional perception, has the personal affect, positive or negative, on the individual. As adventurers, we embrace change for bringing in fresh energy into a withering situation. The actions we take regarding the energy shift, whether positive or negative, can increase or deplete our personal energy. Thoughts of change can drain us through fear and worry. As we internalize this process it accelerates depletion into our bodies. Conversely, if we use change to springboard into faith, positive thought and belief, we refresh and charge our energetic system. This energy cycle is also true of all things in nature. This is why the devastation of a forest fire is necessary for rebirth of the forest. As the mature moves out, it creates room to birth the new into materialization.

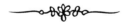

 Insight:

Energy is always in motion. Nothing is static; every moment our world is changing.

Observe constantly that all things take place by change.
– Marcus Aurelius

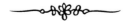

When we are first birthed into this world from infinity our energy is high and pure. We are drawn to babies for their pureness and innocence. Young children who have not filtered their intuition know how to renew their energy. When our thinking mind or ego takes over we rationalize away the connection to source energy.

✉ *You Are the One,*

Just a reminder, the sun rises and sets for you, the mountains, oceans, earth and sky were created just for you.
You are surrounded by beautiful energies just to make your heart sing. Although you may not see me, I am cheering for you! In times of quiet you may even hear me! You are the one that makes my day, every day.

Your Adoring Fan,
  Infinity

Our bodies contain life force energy called Ki, Chi, Prana, or Mana. This life force is what powers our bodies. It is this unseen life force energy which connects us to the universe and replenishes our ability to continue to traverse this material world. It acts as an invisible umbilical cord which connects us to universal life through energy centers or meridians in our human bodies. Just as astronauts need their oxygen tanks to survive in space, we magnificent energies need our connection to universal energy to survive on Earth. When the life force energy or connection to our source ceases to be, our human body dies, and we get re-birthed into the infinite.

Keeping our life force energy connection to the Universe abundant enhances intuitive connection and allows this universal energy to work through us. The lower our life force energy the less physical energy we have.

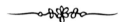

🦋 **Insight:**

Everything in the Universe is energy–including every person, object, thought, word, action and reaction.

The force is what gives the Jedi his power. It's an energy field created by all living things. It surrounds us and penetrates us. It binds the galaxy together.
  – Obi Wan Kenobi, Star Wars

This life force energy is analogous to filling the gas tank in your automobile. One tank of gas will get you so many miles down the road, then you have to fill up again. If you do not fill up the tank, your automobile it will no longer operate. Your personal energy tank is similar. If you do not fill your energy tank, your life force will deplete and your body will no longer operate. When your personal energy tank is low, your body will start leaching energy from itself to keep you going and alive. It will be operating on survival mode, and your outward daily energy level will be very low. Over time, operating in survival mode will cause your physical body to start breaking down becoming ill. Usually, cronic long term illnesses are the result of energy leaching over time. This situation can be reversed in some cases when the body begins getting adequate energy stores if the depletion has not created permanent damage. This can be done with energy work and healing and a change in lifestyle to include replenishing energy.

By focusing on keeping your energy and vibration high, you can slow down the deterioration or oxidation process of the body. Once trained to hold a high energy level, you can learn to project your energy and direct it toward other living objects and give them additional energy. Old world healers and sages are trained to hold, see and direct energy to affect the material world. They understand how the alignment of the energetic world predetermines the material world. Our personal energetic system is very important to our physical well-being and ability to connect to our intuition and destiny. Realizing this energetic cycle gives a fresh perspective on why our thoughts, words and beliefs are so powerful. These are the methods in which we birth new energetic seeds, which grow into material situations and objects as the earthly timeline progresses and the energy materializes into the physical.

Dear Cosmic Seeker,

It is amazing to us that you are not able to feel and sense this energy more clearly as it is plain as day to us. It is what keeps the world and universe in orbit and what keeps the streams moving and the clouds in the sky. Keep looking with your feelings and you may begin to see!

Your Friend,
  Infinity

There are numerous ways to replenish your life force energy. Here are a few examples:

Energy through Higher Range Emotions

When you feel higher range emotions such as love, joy, happiness and contentment, it can increase your energetic vibration and fill your energy tank. The higher your vibration, the closer you are to your connectedness to the universal energy life force.

Laughter instantly fills your energy tank! A good belly laugh each day can keep the low energy away!

Having fun is not overrated!

Remember back in the days of your childhood when everything you did was decided upon by how much fun it would be? It makes no sense to a child why anyone would do anything that is not fun. The days went by freely, easily and joyfully. The laughter and smiles came easily. Laughter of a child is magical. It is real, joyful and comes with ease. When most people hear a child laugh they smile, as they can feel the joyful energy and exuberance abound.

Then you started school. This is where, as the old saying goes, they teach you the 3 R's – reading, 'riting and 'rithmetic. I believe this is also when you began to learn to do things by what was right, responsible, and required, the other 3 R's. Joy or fun was no longer the main consideration in doing anything. The latter 3 R's just seemed to suck the fun out of everything. Now we are older and have lived our lives by the right, responsible and required things and may have even forgotten what having fun and being joyous feels like.

The more consistently you live in the higher range emotions, the clearer your connection becomes. Living in love will fill your tank daily. Have you noticed when you are in love your energy seems boundless? The energy of Appreciation and Gratitude, are a powerful resource. This energy builds your connection to the universe. Appreciate and be grateful for everything, person and circumstance in your life. When you appreciate what you have, the Universe will deliver more for you to appreciate. Starting a daily gratitude journal is one of the most powerful energetic tools you can use. Each day, select 5 things you are grateful for, and jot them down in your journal. Reflect on the goodness, and bask in the appreciation. Do this every day and you will see your life transform toward more to be grateful for!

🦋 Insight:

All power comes from within.

Most powerful is he who has himself in his own power.
   – Seneca

Enthusiasm is contagious, and is an energy builder. When you are with an enthusiastic person you feel better and more enthusiastic yourself. This is why enthusiasm is a top quality of a good sales person. They make you feel good, and when feeling good you will more likely say yes to their product or service.

✉ *Dear Party Animal,*

Yes you! Do you remember how much fun we have together?
The sound of your laughter can make the birds sing!
When the gravity of earth is getting you down . . . get it?
Getting you down . . .gravity (it's a joke, get it?)
Laugh, laugh, laugh . . . laughter will give you instant energy and lift
your spirits . . . spirits . . . HA, ha! Get it? You are THE Spirit!

Always with You in Spirit,
   Infinity

Increasing Energy through Nature

Communing with Nature is a popular and therapeutic way to build energy. The beauty of Mother Earth can replenish your energy. Sitting in the silence of a moonlit night on a sandy shore, under the stars, hearing the power, then feeling the energy of a wave as it engulfs the shore followed by the gentle wave break fills my tank to the brim! Hiking, camping, surfing, and any other time in nature can fill your tank. Seeing a beautiful sunset can fill your tank. The silence of a blanket of snow can fill your tank. You must be present in the now, having an energetic interaction with the wonder of nature to reap the benefits of this energy source – watching a sunset while thinking about work will not likely fill your tank. Again, you must be present to have an energetic exchange with Mother Earth.

Individual Energy Methods

There are also individual deliberate methods to build your energy tank.

Restful sleep increases your energy stores. Sleep increases your life force energy by letting mind or ego out of the way to allow connection to the universe. Notice in times of high energy such as being in love, or being very enthusiastic about something you can live on less sleep and not feel tired. Conversely, notice when you are depressed or in lower range emotions you can sleep all day and still be tired. Sleep is a way to restore your body by eliminating the resistance of the thinking mind or ego to the universal connection which refuels life force energy.

Breathing deeply and deliberately can build your personal energy. Practices like Yoga and Tai Chi also build energy as much of the movement is focused with Breath Work. Increasing life force energy through breath is a powerful practice for many indigenous shaman and healers.

Listening to music that fills your soul can increase your energy stores. Hearing your favorite song can immediately make you feel better, livelier or happier. Sing along and fill your soul!

Including fresh, organic, raw foods in your diet increases your energy tank. The fresher to living the food, the more energizing it is. Increasing energy with raw or natural foods and herbs increases energy.

Creativity builds energy stores. Creativity is derived from a direct inspiration or connection to the Universe or Source Energy and is an energizer. Do anything which feels creative - paint, write, play music, the opportunities are endless!

Find a FUN hobby that will enable you to build enthusiasm and joy and fill your energy tank!

Exercise and move your body! This causes increased breathing and breath work; moving or dancing to your favorite music can be a double energy boost!

Love a furry friend. Pets can increase our feelings of love, happiness and joy! Animals are generally connected to source energy (as they don't have egos to get in the way). The interaction between a pet and owner can be a wonderful source of love and of energy.

Decorate your living space. Living in a beautiful pleasing environment creates energy. Your home should rise up and welcome you joyfully upon your return each day.

Be mindful of the art of placement. The art of Feng Shui, or the art of placement, is derived on this principle of energy flow of a space. It can enhance the placement of rooms, furniture and color in your living space to increase the flow of energy. Daily living in a space designed to enhance the flow of energy is important due to the amount of the exposure of the environment.

Clear the clutter. Clearing out clutter and organizing your home can create energy in previously stagnant areas of your home. Discard items that no longer bring you joy. Remove broken things, things you are keeping only out of obligation, or things which do not evoke a positive, happy feeling. Take down old pictures, chachkies, and simplify.

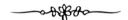

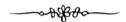 Insight:

Keep your life force energy high and focus on what you want to bring into your life. Energy goes where attention flows.

My mind is a garden. My thoughts are the seeds. My harvest will be either flowers or weeds.
– Mel Weldon

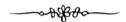

Depleting Energy

Increasing your energy, or filling your tank, is one side of the equation. Keeping and conserving your energy also helps to keep your energy tank full. The following can deplete your energy.

Beware of the vampires!

Energy vampires are exhausting. They replenish their personal energy tank by taking energy from others. It is cosmic siphoning of life force energy. They can have explosive or volitle personalities. After exploding on you they are energized, leaving you feeling in the lower vibrations of hurt, anger, or frustration. They can constantly complain, or live in drama. They tell you every detail and can turn your good mood into a tired one. You become tired because they have depleted you of your energy. Constantly being around someone like this can reduce your energy to the point of causing chronic illness. Disassociating yourself may be the only way to protect your energy. The energy vampire will likely move on to another victim then. They will often select a few victims to attack, while being pleasing and pleasurable to others.

⊠ My Little Precious,

Beware of the Vampires that want to suck your life force energy.
Cosmically they want your energy, in the physical they want your blood.
Either way, if they get you – over time you are gone. Game over.

Your Batty Friend,
  Infinity

P.S. Beware, they always come disguised in nice packages at first.

- Eating highly processed foods, and food with chemical additives depletes energy. Not getting life force energy through living food, your body will start leaching energy from itself to keep you going and alive.
- Living in a cluttered and unclean environment lowers energy. Clutter creates stagnant energy. Each time you look at the clutter or area which needs cleaning it drains your energy. You know you should clear out the area. You know you should clean up. Each time you see the broken clock you think I need to fix it. Fix it or get rid of it. It is robbing you of your valuable energy!
- Pessimism lowers energy levels through the emotional drain of focusing on lack.
- Excessive TV watching lowers energy levels. It disengages our connectedness to people and true emotion. It can create addictive behavior to divert our connection to intuition.
- Excessive exposure to electrical fields can lower energy levels. Living near power lines, cell towers, or with too many electronic gadgets all the time can lower energy.
- Complaining and retelling old war stories, can lower energy by keeping you in lack.
- Lower range emotions can lower energy. Worry depletes energy. Fearfulness depletes energy.

- Remaining in lower vibrating emotions for extended periods depletes energy.

Your body will naturally attempt to increase energy stores. For example, sleeping all day is a sign of depression – a lower vibrating emotion. It is the body's response toward attempting to increase depleted energy stores through restful sleep.

Again, everything is energy, and every interaction we have with anything else is energy. Every interaction with another person, place or thing gives or takes your energy. An interaction can give both participants energy, or can drain energy from both. It is not a linear exchange. It is important to be aware of your energy field and notice the energy exchanges in your daily life.

For example, a personal relationship can enhance one, both or none of the partners. To attract higher vibrating, energy giving interactions you must keep your own energy high.

 Insight:

Energy vibrates and attracts in the same frequency, which resonates with it.

The happiness of your life depends on the quality of your thoughts.
– Marcus Aurelius

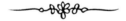

You can actually change the outcome of a situation by managing your energy level.

One day on my way home from work I decided to stop at the grocery store. As I maneuvered my way around a corner there was a lady with her cart blocking the entire isle. I waited for a minute, hoping she would notice and tuck her cart to one side, allowing me to get by. She seemed to notice, and did not move. By this time there were a couple of us waiting to get by. I nicely said, "Excuse me." She glared back at me and said, "I suppose if you were me you would move your cart." Without hesitation or anger I said, "Absolutely." She moved her cart with an attitude and I walked by. My first reaction was to lower my vibration to match her vibration of grumpiness, and silently think "what is her problem?" I stopped this reaction and decided to keep my vibration high and energetically offer her love and compassion. At I shopped in the next aisle, this same lady came down the aisle chasing me down to apologize for her rudeness. Her vibration was now quite noticeably raised as she smiled and thanked me for making her day! I smiled as I accepted her gratitude. As I continued to shop I noticed her smiling at strangers, being friendly to the clerk and other shoppers, she even let someone with a smaller purchase go ahead of her in line. This is the power of energy work!

Try this experiment yourself the next time and have FUN!

⊠ *Dear Chameleon,*

Just for fun . . . and it is all about the fun! Increase your energy level and see how your interactions change your surroundings. You are a reverse chameleon! See how your happy energy changes everything. Don't worry be happy!

Your Loving Friend,
  Infinity

Being aware of your own personal energy level is important to your energetic health.

Learn to live in a place of higher vibration and hold your energy tank in a full position. Like a protective shield, this energy will reduce all the negative static from the world around you.

Situations, which in the past dropped your emotions into fear and anger, will no longer affect you this way. You are in control of your emotional perception and are utilizing your navigational system! In time, these situations will no longer happen to you, or exist in your reality.

Focusing energy through words, thoughts and beliefs; and through using your emotional navigational system through positive perception is a core element of manifesting into the material reality. Keeping your levels high through the methods mentioned above bring you to a clearer connection to your intuition, and defends against cosmic amnesia which hampers discovering your greatness on earth. Through your intuition you will be able to tap into the infinite power of the Universe. With this comes great freedom as you rise up and fill yourself with joy and fulfillment. You will achieve freedom from the world of materialism, into the world of creation. The sky is the limit. Everything you want can and will be yours.

Chapter 5:
The Art of Intuition

Have you ever had a gut feeling about something? Most of us believe there is an inner knowing each of us possesses. We will call this voice your knowing self. It is the part of you that remembers you are a powerful, magnificent, positive energy. Your knowing self is the you before you came to play this Awakening Destiny adventure on Earth. Every adventurer has a cheering section led by the Universe, and your knowing self. Your fans may include your angels, guides, ancestors and more. They want you to win the game. Your intuition is your connection to the universe and all your raving fans - giving you insights on remembering your magnificence, finding your destiny, and winning the game. Once you can hear your intuition, you can better traverse this material terrain with the help of your cosmic 'home team' – the Universe. Let's say you know you have an intuition or knowing self. The big question is – do you hear and act upon your intuitive messages? Do you know what your intuition sounds like?

Tune into the channel of your knowing self, and let your intuition help you to create what you desire. Imagine wanting to hear a program on FM radio, but you are tuned into AM radio. Although you have your radio turned on, you will never hear the program. You are tuning into a different frequency. You may think the program is just not there. In reality, the program is being broadcast, but you just can't hear it. You need to tune your radio to the proper frequency, or vibration to hear it.

This is the same with your intuition.

You need to be at a certain frequency, or vibration to hear it.

 Insight:

Do not busy your mind with trivial thought or mind chatter. Hear and tune in to the feeling place of your intuition deliberately.
Be alone with your thoughts on a daily basis.

Only in solitude do we find ourselves.
 – Miguel de Unamuno y Jugo

Living in a state of positive emotion, increases your vibration or frequency to match your intuitive voice. The lower your vibrational frequency, the more 'static' interferes and you will be less likely to hear your intuition.

✉ *Hello All of You Fans,*

Tune in the vibration of radio station ME. Raise your vibration through good feeling emotions and you will be able to clear the static and tune in.
I know it sounds weird, trust me, these tunes will be music to your ears! Tune in to hear the guidance of your adoring fans!

Your Rockin' DJ,
 Daddy I

Your high range emotions such as joy, love, appreciation, empowerment, and enthusiasm bring you to the frequency or higher vibration to tune into your intuition. These higher vibrating emotions also create a portal for clearer communication with your intuition. Creating this clear channel with your intuition is a critical part of traversing with spirit in spite of earth's material terrain. This connection allows the universe to deliver all the information needed for you to overcome your cosmic amnesia. You increase your intuitive connection by continuously looking for the best feeling you can for a given situation. The better you feel, the closer you come to the frequency necessary to receiving your intuition. The lower range emotions such as fear, depression, powerlessness, hate, envy, guilt, anger and worry all lower your vibrational frequency and bring you further from hearing your intuition and realizing your shining powerful destiny.

✉ *Our Dearest Fun Lover,*

Do you hear your raving fans? Listen closely and you will.
Know we are always with you, so close we could touch you – if we were physical, of course. Remember yesterday, when it felt like someone was guiding you?
Don't tell anyone, but yes, it was Me.

Keeping My Eyes Wide Open,
Infinity

Intuitive information can arrive as a feeling, words, images in a dream, or pictures in your mind.

Intuitive information is assimilated in three primary ways; seeing, hearing and feeling. Most people use a combination of all three.

Each of us can access our intuition, some more easily than others. For most, the connection with intuition becomes muffled as we are taught the linear, logical, thinking mind is correct. This usually happens when we, as children, enter school and are forced into believing logic is the way of the world. When our intuitive voice opposes logical thought we are taught to ignore intuition.

As the voice of logic grows in our minds, it drowns out the voice of intuition. Some describe hearing their intuition as a whisper. Your intuition will get stronger and louder as you continue to open this doorway through continuing to listen and act on your intuitive messages.

Intuition extends awareness. Everything is a sign.

Some hear intuition. They can hear thoughts and interpret them. Intuitive insights may come as words spoken, or as hearing more in a conversation than is spoken. Your intuition may come to you in a feeling. There are many expressions such as "It just felt right," or "I had a sinking feeling in my stomach," or "Something made me feel creepy." Your intuition may come to you symbolically, through pictures in your mind or images in a dream.

Intuition can also come in the form of synchronicity. Synchronicity is when seemly random events align to a desired result. This is more commonly referred to as a coincidence. When accessing the multidimensional, spiritual world – nothing is a coincidence. Life becomes an adventure when following your intuition and going with what the universe presents to you.

 Insight:

Synchronicity is a major clue that you are on the path.

Intuition is perception via the unconscious.
– Carl Jung

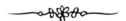

In the whole of the universe all things are possible. The universe operates multi-dimensionally, and your intuition can help to traverse through the linear limitation and open you to unlimited possibilities. Intuition can lead you to your perfect partner, career, house, anything you desire in this material world. Once you have created the desire, and have aligned your energy through alignment of your thoughts, words and beliefs- the power of the universe goes into action. Belief again is the big one here. You must believe you are worthy and able to attain your desire.

Your universal cheering section communicates to you through your intuition. Your million dollar idea is awaiting your discovery. Your perfect mate is awaiting your chance meeting. Your perfect life is awaiting you in your future. All you have to do is tune into the frequency of your intuition and allow the unfolding.

Mindfulness – The Power of Now

Mindfulness is the practice of being in the moment. It is the practice of paying attention to the details of each moment and living in the now. Enjoying the details of how the bird sings, and flower blooms.

The opposite of mindfulness is mindlessness. Mindlessness is going through each day on autopilot. Doing the same old thing without a thought. When what your physical body is doing and what your mind is thinking are not in harmony.

Most people prize themselves on multi-tasking. The more things you can do in a day, or in a moment, the more successful and efficient you are. Our linear world and ego prides itself on how much more we can get accomplished. Our minds are always racing to the next thing. We are driving home from work thinking about the unfinished project or plans for the weekend. We are helping the kids with homework while cooking dinner and talking to our spouse on the phone.

In our harried world, mindfulness takes practice and is of utmost importance to being in the flow of intuition.

The lesson of mindfulness has two power points.

Power point 1:

It is only in the now when you are able to hear and act on your intuition and intuitive hunches.

Your intuition operates right now. It does not live in the past or project into the future. The power to hear and feel your intuition is only now. Every moment, in the moment, your intuition is guiding you.

The power to act upon your intuition is now. When you begin to tune into the vibration of your intuition you will get ideas and hunches for inspired action. Your intuition is guiding you toward this inspired action to take now.

It is not something to contemplate or mull over.

Inspired action is taking a leap of faith today.
Everyone has heard someone's, maybe even your own "If only" story.
If only I had taken a chance on my hunch and bought that right stock.
If only I went with the feeling to turn, I would have avoided the accident.
If only . . . You fill in the blank.
Take inspired action on your intuitive hunches today, even on the smallest details. Your dreams will begin to unfold beautifully, right before your eyes.

Power point 2:

Right now is your only point of creation; the only point where your action can affect your future outcomes.

Your emotions, thoughts and words you choose to use right now, create your future.
Realize that the power of Now is everything.
It is most important to be aware of your feelings and emotions in each now.

Fully experience what is happening today, and take action based on your intuitive hunches. Keep your thoughts always pointed toward the life you are creating.

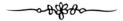

🦋 **Insight:**

Now is the only point of power and connection to your knowing self, and most importantly, it is your only point of creation using your intuition.

The secret of health for both mind and body is not to mourn the past, not to worry about the future, not to anticipate troubles, but to live the present moment wisely and earnestly.
– Buddha

Your future outcomes are a manifestation of what you are creating in the Now, and now is the only point of contact with your intuition.

Everything manifesting in your physical world now, is a result of your thoughts, words and emotions from the past. This is why taking action based on your current circumstance is not effective in changing your life and simply holds you the same energy.

Taking action based on your intuitive connection takes you toward the life you desire.

Intuitive connection is a foundational element in your Awakening Destiny challenge.

Train your mind toward the positive perception of your current circumstance to raise your emotional frequency to make your intuitive connection.

Silence is Golden

Silence is far more than the absence of sound. It is also the absence of thought and activity. Although on the surface, silence appears to be the absence of the physical stimulation, it is far from empty. The silence of mind creates a space in which all things are possible. It creates the potential to birth greatness. Intuition comes from silence. Silence is the making of space for receiving. Silence is a state of mind, in addition to physical surroundings.

One can be sitting at the top of a mountain, thinking thoughts and feelings, which fill the space without words. With excessive thoughts, there is no space for silence although there is no sound. Conversely, one can be in the middle of a bustling town and be in complete silence through the training of emptying the mind. From silence you can move in any direction, and possibilities abound. Silence can be obtained through solitude or meditation. Silence is created by going inward within self and by being present to the stillness of mind, body, emotion and thought.

We live in a society, which does not value silence. The squeaky wheel gets the oil. It covets busyness as aliveness even though empty with mindless action. We use sound as companionship to drown out loneliness or emptiness. Know that silence is neither lonely nor empty. Once mastered it will become what you the superhero needs to enhance your super spidey senses.

Using Breath work and meditation:
Deep rhythmic breathing moves more oxygen into the blood. Higher levels of oxygen affect the brain by lengthening and slowing its waves to a lower state of Alpha. Indigenous shamans of many cultures use breathing to increase their power or energy for healing or seeing.

The key to both increasing energy and meditation is breathing. Meditation is the emptying of ones mind to allow silence and intuition.

Courageous is Your Soul

The mission should you choose to accept it, will take the courage of a superhero. As you begin to walk the path of intuition, other adventurers who have not yet awakened, will say you are crazy. You will likely be going against the grain of linear thought. You may decide to quit a secure job and start up a business. You may decide to leave the security of a relationship to free yourself of toxic energy. You may decide to move to another country. You may decide to shed everything you own and give it to charity. Whatever your multi-dimensional destiny you will be on your way, and those who knew the linear you will be aghast at your irrational behavior.

On a beautiful, sunny summer day while enjoying the day at the beach, we set out crab nets at the end of the pier. Every so often, we would pull up the nets to reveal our catch. We collected the crab in a bucket adding more as the day progressed. Throughout the day as a crab tried to climb out of the bucket, the other crab would pull him back in. The bucket was not very deep, and eventually one would make it to the top and get pulled back in. They would climb on another's back to try to be the one at the top of the heap, only to get pulled back down.

This is quite an analogy for un-awakened adventurers thinking linearly, each trying to get to the top of heap on the back of others only to get pulled back down into the reality of the bucket. Perhaps the security of the known situation in the bucket keeps them pulling each other back in. Little do the crab know there is a world to discover and freedom beyond the bucket. Don't let others fears and worries pull you back down into the safe bucket you know and want to break free from. Be courageous! Try something new at every opportunity. Go beyond the limits of your current reality.

🦋 **Insight:**

Have the courage to go beyond the limits of your current reality.

Whatever you do, you need courage. Whatever course you decide on, there is always someone to tell you that you are wrong. There are always difficulties arising that tempt you to believe your critics are right.

– Ralph Waldo Emerson

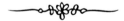

Connection with your intuition is a powerful element in overcoming your cosmic amnesia and remembering your greatness.

✉ *Beautiful Adventurer,*

Do you want to know how to be in the flow of the universe?
It is so simple you overlooked it the first time – Have Fun!!
Have Fun and Feel the Flow!

Your Universal Plumber,
  Infinity

Take action upon your intuition. Have faith in your intuition. Your intuition is your higher self, and the voice of your infinite cheering team. Your higher self knows the destiny card you have selected. Hearing and taking action on your intuitive guidance will lead you toward the life you desire to create. Use your emotions as the navigator. Go with what feels good and makes you feel abundant. Above all, have fun and know you are on your way!

Chapter 6:
Befriending Your Ego

Okay, what is the ego? It sounds like a weird psychological thing. And what does that have to do with me discovering my destiny? Is logic overrated? Ha, another mind blower. The ego is another challenge placed in the game. Some spiritual teachings have really depicted the ego as something bad that keeps us from realizing our spiritual fullness. Simply, the ego is the tool of the material world. Just as your intuition, through emotion, is the tool of the world of creation. One is not better than the other. They both exist within you. Ego is not bad, something to be ignored, or conquered. It is just what is.

Initially, the ego helps us to traverse the material world by helping us assimilate into a society of materialness. It helps us differentiate ourselves, and be separate from other adventurers. Ego helps us to survive on the earthly plane. It strives to conquer, be the best, the most powerful, have the most, as this is the way to survival on this plane. Ego creates the lower vibrating emotions of worry, fear, and some of the pitfalls such as envy, drama, etc. Ego strives to keep us separated from one another. Ego is the survival tool of the material world. Communicating with your intuition is the tool of the world of creation. The beauty is the wonderful contrast, by transcending the material world into the world of creation, you become a creator of the material world. Another great twist of this grand adventure!!

Learning to befriend and live symbionically with your ego is a reward of the adventure. How wonderful this is! Ego provides the contrast which helps guide you to a better feeling place and to create your road map.

Ego provides the spice in the game, and the wonderful contrast, which is one of the many reasons you wanted to play the game in the first place!

Remember, ego functions in the material world and intuition functions in the world of creation. Most of your life, up to now, has likely been spent learning to listen to your ego since you were learning to traverse in the material world.

Now you are a student of the world of creation and must learn to listen to your intuition. The voice, or feeling, of your intuition must become louder than the voice of your ego.

Your limiting beliefs can also be a result of your ego attempting to keep you safe for survival. Ego has created a belief system, or blueprint, of how to properly survive the material world.

Earlier you discovered your emotional navigation system. Turn on your system and you will find your limiting beliefs.

When you have positive beliefs the seeds you are growing in this area make you happy.

The area in your life that is lower on the happiness scale is most likely the area in which you have the most limiting beliefs. This area probably causes the most worry, fear or anxiety for you.

The ego attempts to maintain control through the use of lower vibrating emotions such as worry, fear, anxiety and guilt. Most of your life, up to now, has likely been spent learning to listen to your ego and learning to traverse in the material world by avoiding feeling these emotions. As creators we acknowledge and embrace these feelings as an indication from our navigational system to turn our thoughts to the better feeling emotion.

Your Ego Voice

When you first arrived into the Adventurer's game you were dropped into this material world, based on the circumstances card you selected in the cosmos. Your earthly family had learned how to traverse this terrain, and from the day you were born started teaching you what they knew. They taught you to watch out for strangers who may hurt you, hold hands when crossing the street or you may be killed, beware of dogs that may bite you, fire may burn you, and on and on. These are fundamental guidelines to survive in your human body vehicle, basic care and maintenance issues. They know that these things have happened to other adventurer's in the past and they died. Basically, death is a word meaning – game over.

 *Dear Adventurer,*

Your magnificent cosmic self will never die, just your earth vehicle. Yup, then you will be standing in line again waiting for another chance. Of course, there is always another chance! Death – what an ego trip!

Eternally Yours,
Infinity

Some ego lessons of survival are very important if you want to remain in the game. When an adventurer becomes deeply rooted in the material world, they may no longer hear their intuitive voice of universal love, joy and magnificence. These adventurers become deeply entrenched in the material world, and the ego's quest for survival may go to the extent of extreme separateness of other adventurers.

 Insight:

The Ego was never meant to take the lead. The ego is meant to exist in harmony with your knowing self, providing polarity and contrast, to increase desire toward the world of creation.

The gem cannot be polished without friction, nor man perfected without trials.
  – Confucius

There is an increased challenge when the ego becomes so deeply rooted. The adventurer loses his awareness of his greater magnificence. When this happens the ego becomes dominant and will try to rule their earthly experience. This causes an imbalance, and can lead to further separation from creation, and your destiny card.

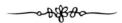

 Dear Speed Racer,

Know which Flagman is directing your car. Intuition will take you to the finish line. Ego will send you around the track backwards – the joke is you will think you are winning the race.

Cheering You Toward the Trophy,
  Infinity

The ego, in its very nature, tries to take control. As the Universe has tools toward creation, the ego has tools to keep you rooted in the material world. This keeps you further from the world of creation. The ego utilizes its arsenal of tools to keep you rooted in materialism. The tools of the ego are also the pitfalls to the adventure.

Here are a few tools of the ego or pitfalls you may recognize.

Greed

Greed and need for more materialism is a powerful pitfall of the game. The need to obtain more bling is a result of ego control. Needing the latest and greatest, biggest and baddest stuff to feel important or successful keeps you rooted in materialism. There is a fine line between material greed of the ego, and creating the world of your desires through inspiration. Although, the big house, fancy car, and material stuff seem the same on the outside, the difference is the feeling behind acquiring the stuff.

When you acquire the stuff to keep up with the neighbors, to flaunt your success and let others know you have made it, or to prove your worthiness or power you have succumbed to the tool of the ego- greed.

By contrast, when you understand the standard of success in life isn't in the thing, you have entered the world of creation. It isn't the money or the stuff you acquire which indicates success. It is absolutely the amount of joy, love and appreciation you feel which makes you successful.

You can have the big house, fancy car and loads of money and absolutely be in the flow of your destiny. Or you can have the big house, fancy car and loads of money and absolutely be stuck in a pitfall of the ego. Again it is not about the stuff. It is just an illusion of the material world. The only opinion that matters is your own, and material stuff exists only to bring you joy and help you create your life of passion and to fulfill your destiny. Whether you live in a mansion, loft or cave; create what best suits your life, without regard to the opinions of others. It is the essence of your feeling behind the stuff that is the difference.

🦋 Insight:

It is not about the stuff. It is the feeling behind acquiring the big house, or fancy car that is the difference between living by ego, or living by creation.

If we worry too much about ourselves, we won't have time for others.
– Mother Teresa

Competition

All competition is based on the premise of lack. Supposing there is not enough to go around so we must be the best and get there first. We learn at a very young age that competition is the way society rates winners and losers. The concept of most sports is based on winning and losing. The winners celebrate and the losers hang their heads in defeat.

Pretentious, boastful, or conceited behavior is also a result of competition. This is the result of ego control. Remember this litmus test, if it feels good, and brings you joy whether you win or lose it is creation based. If you feel even a smidgen worse, or inadequate when you lose, it is ego and competition based. Let go of competition and singleness and embrace the concept of oneness with the universe.

Power

Power is one of those sneaky pitfalls. In this world of consistent duality, there is a fine line with power. Leadership can be a tool of creation. Authoritarianism is a power trip of the ego. Freedom is an element of creation. Dictatorship is an element of ego. Many times the dichotomy is two sides of the same coin.

✉ *Dear Eternal Winner,*

You know there are no losers in the cosmos. Maybe it's the atmosphere on earth, which causes beautiful, shining, pure energy beings to think they could possibly even be losers. How absurd! We cannot even imagine it. You are a brave soul to play this game!
What a mind trip!

Your Biggest Fan,
    Infinity

Hearing Your Intuition vs. Ego

Training yourself to hear and trust your intuition will develop over time. The more you act on your intuition, the stronger your connection will become. One of the reasons you may doubt, discount, or flat out not listen to your intuition is what I call a pitfall of the game.

So what are these pitfalls?

These pitfalls are distractions of the ego to your intuitive voice.

These distractions come in the form of greed, envy, gossip, drama, blame, and others. Remember, these ego distractions are pitfalls that you programmed into your game.

Just imagine the universe has a deck of pitfall cards – just for fun, of course.

So for example, let's say you are happily going about your day. Then you see someone in a sleek, black, luxurious, convertible sportscar, and this triggers a pitfall –the envy card. This card distracts you from the moment by making you feel envious of the person driving the car. You think something like, why is he driving that car? How can he really afford that car anyway? I bet he thinks he is pretty cool in that car.

You immediately go to the emotion of envy or jealousy. This lowers your vibration.

Wow, what an interesting turn of events. In a moment, you went from being happy and focused in the moment, to envy, then jealousy. All this happened because you saw a physical object, the car, which triggered a pitfall.

Do you see how these pitfalls work? Pretty sneaky, huh? Pitfalls usually lead to the lower vibrating emotions of worry, fear and lack. In the example above, the pitfall of envy, led to the emotion of jealousy and to the feeling of lack.

Why are they called pitfalls? They lower your vibration and connection to your intuition is impaired, thus is a pitfall to awakening your destiny.

✉ Dear Ever Seeking Adventurer

You set up pitfalls in your game to make it more challenging to hear and follow your intuition. After all, how challenging would your journey be if someone whispered all the secrets to win directly in your ear? Ha! Remember you can live in harmony with your ego—just keep your eyes focused on creation!

Infinity

Tools of the Universe

These tools are feelings or techniques we can focus on to overcome the pitfalls in your experience. Here are some examples:

Let's take the pitfall card of envy. When you feel envy toward the person driving the sleek, black, luxurious convertible sportscar, acknowledge the pitfall.

Recognize the trigger – the car.

Embrace it – could it be you want a car like this?

If so, make the intention to create it in your life, get excited! You know you can create anything you want in your life. You have identified the pitfall and can now overcome it.

Gratitude is a tool, which you can use to neutralize the pitfall of envy.

The moment you feel envious of someone, think of something in your life for which you are grateful. Feel the gratitude throughout your body.

Let the wonderful state of gratitude wash over you.

Here are some other common pitfalls and tools.

Pitfall: Greed
Tool: Give. Give of your time and resources.

Greed cannot exist within the context of the abundance and giving.
Greed is an insatiable need to control your physical world.
Greed is born from the belief that physical resources are limited.
Everyone can create unlimited resources, everything they desire. Our Universe is abundant.

Pitfall: Gossip
Tool: Silence. Know the creation power of your words. Words are a powerful tool for creation- use them wisely.

Eliminate Gossip from your life. Gossip keeps you stuck in the drama of nothingness. Keep your thoughts and words positive and forward thinking.

Pitfall: Drama

Tool: Awareness. Know that you are living in this moment, which was created by your words, thoughts and feelings of yesterday. Balance this energy and release the focus on your circumstance, and begin creating your perfect tomorrow with your words, thoughts and feelings today.

Release the need for drama in your life. This drama keeps you rooted to where you are, unable to master the art of creation.

Pitfall: Blame

Tool: Forgiveness. Forgiving others is the greatest gift you can give yourself. Release this energy, and it will release you.

Let go of Blame. Blaming others for events in your life creates a victim mentality. This will keep you in the bondage of past events.

Some may believe ego's pitfalls are bad, leading them to deduce ego is bad. On the contrary, ego provides the great contrast, which leads you to the desires of your creation. Pitfalls may be useful to provide contrast to bring our desires into our awareness. In the example of the car, the pitfall of envy may be useful to identify the joy owning a similar car may bring. The ultimate immunity challenge in this adventure is identifying the pitfalls, and using the proper creation tool to overcome it. Feel it, recognize the feeling and move through it. The key is to not stay stuck in the pitfall.

As you travel on your journey you will discover powerful creating tools to overcome ego's tools or pitfalls of creation. The good news is for every pitfall there is a tool from the Universe to overcome it.

✉ *Dear Ever Seeking Adventurer*

Just learned about the pitfall card, huh? I know, the pitfalls seem like a bummer. They are really designed to make the game more fun. Never fear! We would not leave you to fend for yourself with those sneaky pitfalls. Look for tools from the Universe to overcome those pitfalls!

Tools, baby, Tools . . . that's what we have for you. Keep listening to your intuition so you may add them to your toolbox.

Your Handyman,
    Infinity

Ego and Self Esteem

Seeking approval of others is perhaps the first pitfall we learn in this adventure. We learn as young children to seek approval of other players. We seek the approval of our parents, teachers, friends and occasionally even strangers. We wear designer fashions, keep up with the Joneses, climb the corporate ladder, and strive to get all the spelling words right on the test to earn the gold star. The gold star which shows the world you are accepted and met with someone's approval. In the material world, it feels really good to be accepted and feels really bad to feel rejected. In the world of creation, your internal knowing is the only acceptance that is needed. Because you exist, you know you are always accepted. There is no doubt you are pure positive, magnificent energy, and nothing can take that away from you. Know your divine magnificence and do not seek the approval of others. Do not accept their acclaim, accolades or approval. Accepting approval in the good times, give others the power to take away the same when they decide it so. Know it is more about their need than you. They cannot take away, what you do not own.

 Insight:

Pitfalls are rooted in the material world. Tools from the Universe are rooted in the world of creation. We learn to overcome the pitfalls of the material world when we transcend into the world of creation.

Enthusiasm will not mix with fear, envy, greed, jealousy, doubt, revenge, hatred, intolerance and procrastination.
    – Napoleon Hill

The Random House definition of self-esteem is, a realistic respect for or favorable impression of oneself, self-respect. Conversely, low self-esteem is an unfavorable impression of oneself and low self-respect.

Low self-esteem is the result of seeking approval of others to the extent it undermines your own approval of yourself. Simply stated, the player cares more about what other players think of them, than what they think of themselves.

You may have been told as a child that thinking of yourself first is selfish.

Beginning today, I give you permission (and you know you don't need my permission, right?) to be selfish. From this day forward, regard how you think, and feel first, before you regard how anyone else will think and feel. Guilt about being selfish is a tool of the ego, and a pitfall of creation. All great creators are selfish and selfless. In their selfishness and selflessness they bring their great destiny to the world as a gift.

Ego and the Power of Now

As you may recall, now is your great and only moment of creation. Right now is your only point of creation. Now is when you are able to hear and act on your intuition and intuitive hunches. It is only in the now, that you are able to access your powerful ability toward creation. You choose in each moment to move toward creation, or do nothing and move toward ego or material existence. Ego operates as the opposite of creation. Ego's goal is for you to remain unaware and unfocused on the now, since this is your only point of creation.

Ego wants you to focus on everything except now, such as the past, or future.

Focusing on the past usually comes in the form of reliving memories. Constantly thinking, talking about, and referring to the past hold you there in the past. Sometimes it is disguised as reliving through thought and feeling pleasing memories of the good old days. Thinking and talking about the past keeps you in that space. You are occupying the current now with events of the past, which keeps you from acting right now in the present. Sometimes bad memories of the past are disguised as anger, hurt or pain and live through being unforgiving. Being unforgiving holds you in the past, and keeps you from realizing the great creator you are. You may have heard when you forgive someone it is more for you than for the forgiven. It is true. You set yourself free of the control of the ego and the past through forgiveness. Forgiveness does not mean you must forget, it means to release its hold, by accepting the greater good in life.

✉ *Dear Creator,*

Wow, the ego - what a 'head game' – oh yeah, I forgot, it IS the head game. What a joke! I know you are too cool to fall for ego's mind tricks. It must be a blast playing though!

Your Greatest Admirer,
Infinity

Land Mines of Fear and Worry

Living fearlessly means learning to navigate away from the landmines of fear and worry, two of egos greatest tools and creations biggest pitfalls.

Both fear and worry are created by ego creating the vision of the worst case scenario in your powerful now.

Conversely, to overcome fear and worry you must begin living in the now.

Pay attention to what is occurring in the now, and live fully in this moment. The only time you should take your focus off the now is to envision positively the perfect destination you are creating. Each day, move in the direction of this destination.

Have faith and know you will arrive at your destination safely, and the world will be yours! You will fulfill your destiny and win your game.

🦋 Insight:

At any one moment, fear and Faith cannot live inside you at the same time. Ask yourself which you will choose.

Faith is the great motive power, and no man realizes his full possibilities unless he has the deep conviction that life is eternally important and that his work well done is a part of an unending plan.
– Calvin Coolidge

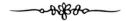

The ego keeps us connected to the material world. Our creative mind, or intuition, keeps us connected to the infinite world of creation. These are two separate worlds – one living linearly, and one in the multidimensional infinite beyond. The action of living from each world is at opposite ends of the spectrum. When you are rooted in the material, ego controls your actions, and you move further from creation. The ego depletes your energy and leads you toward the negative creation cycle, which lowers your vibrational frequency to intuition. The ego operates from experiences in the past, or the past experiences of others, projected into the future. The ego cannot understand or accept the world of creation. The ego's job is to keep you rooted in the material world, based on past experience to keep you safe within its limited boundaries.

When you train your mind toward the positive, intuition controls your actions, and the material world has diminishing power over you. You become the master of the material world, of ego, and it is not the master of you. Training your mind requires focus and awareness. Your mind is accustomed to letting the ego run your life. To regain knowledge of your magnificence you must reign in your ego. Befriending your ego realizes and welcomes ego's role of polarity in the game.

How sweet it is!!

Chapter 7:
Manifesting Material Wealth and Success

Who wants to be a millionaire? This sounds like a popular game show. More accurately the question may be "How do I become a millionaire?"

Here we probably get to the crux of what most adventurers want to know.

Money is an area where bridging the material world is the most apparent. Since this subject is so emotionally charged, your inherent belief system is a huge determining factor in your achieving financial success. Many financial gurus say, you will be in the earnings bracket of your five closest friends, because they keep you rooted in the money belief of that bracket. Each earning bracket talks, thinks and believes in a certain way. We are generally trained to be around those who are like us. To become successful at something new, you need to be with those who are successful doing that thing. They help to change your belief system and learn new skills. As a newly found superhero, dare to change your belief system to bigger loftier goals.

Tom's first recollection of money is that it really grew on trees! Exuberantly pumping the petals of his shiny red bicycle with the gooseneck handle bars and glitter blue banana seat, feeling real freedom with the wind blowing upon his face, abundance abounded all around him. He loved riding his bike! Riding his wheels under a tree, reaching up into the air and grabbing a handful of leaves pretending it was money. He really believed it was money! Dreaming of all the cool gadgets to buy and things to do with his never-ending supply of the green stuff. He gave it away to friends and spent it generously. This was the life! The green stuff really felt like money and he felt like a millionaire! This all changed when Tom was 11. He got terribly sick with pneumonia and was hospitalized for a week. Once he was well enough, he was able to return home. One night, behind his desk paying bills, Tom's dad made a comment about the hospital bill being overwhelmingly expensive. He looked unhappy and stressed. Tom did not want to cause his Dad unhappiness. He wished he didn't have to go the hospital. He wished there was no hospital bill. He realized money did not grow on trees. In that moment, he felt unworthy of this money, which caused his Dad to furrow his brow. Subconsciously, money and success became a driving force to regain his worthiness and make his Dad proud. A workaholic, he climbed the corporate ladder. His drive to work harder increased with each promotion and raise. His life became unbalanced and unhappy, and it was apparent, regardless of the size of his paycheck, it would never be enough.

A key to remember in this chapter is that most of what we have learned about acquiring material wealth and success, is taught to us by our family pod and our life experiences. We will have to assess these beliefs and be willing to unlearn these lessons, if needed. First, take a look at the person or people who gave you the advice on which you built your beliefs. Have they learned to master wealth and success? Are they living a life filled with abundance and passion? If not, there is a good chance you have some unlearning or changing of your of financial blueprint to do.

✉ *Dear Surfrider,*

Whoo-hoo!! You are onto the wildest part of the ride! You are riding the crest of the wave! Learning to override your old ego mindset on material creation is the changing point in your adventure. Hang on to your board and hang ten . . . here we go!!!

Your Big Kahuna,
    Infinity

Today, most societies judge success by how much you can acquire materially. Most of what we acquire is by earning money, saving or splurging, depending on your blueprint, and buying what you desire. Our ego will also have us believe more is better. Therefore, the bigger house, faster or sleeker car is better. The more bling the better.

Once your ego starts chasing a tangible symbol is has attached to wealth to produce a desired feeling, when the goal is achieved and the feeling is not produced the target will change and move to more, bigger, badder or better – continuing to chase the desired feeling.

This is all well and good. You may want a bigger house, sleeker car, or more bling. However, by associating these material items with your self worth, you put a judgment on them. Having them is good, not having them is bad, interpreted as if you have them you are a winner, and if you don't have them you are a loser. HA!! How much further from the truth can this be?

Most of what we have learned about acquiring the material is ego controlled. The ego will have you believe the path to material success is to do something. What is the success?

Napoleon Hill defines success: Success is the development of the power with which to get whatever one wants in life without interfering with the rights of others.

Studies show up to 95% of the population work a job they don't like just for the paycheck. They tolerate the working during the week to make it to the weekend to have fun and do what they enjoy doing.

What if success is assessed by how many hours you spend of life in fulfillment, happiness and joy instead of making a living and acquiring material possessions? What if success were based on whether you are able to live in the highest of emotional vibration all the time?

✉ *Dear Rock Star,*

You are a magnificent, pure positive energy. Having a lot of bling does not make you better, and most of all not having the bling will never take away your greatness. You are great just because you exist!
Keep on rocking!

Your Groupie,
   Infinity

Money and material wealth are not required to live your live with passion. Mother Teresa for example, lived a very modest passion filled life. The turnabout is to seek doing what you enjoy and are passionate about and discovering through intuition the action to manifest financial freedom. Money gives you the freedom to define how you want to spend your time. Money freedom gives you more time to do what you enjoy. Joyful living raises your vibration to hear the intuitive guidance and collaborate with the universe to live your destiny card. It is easier to allow destiny to unfold when you have the time freedom to do what you love, regardless of money. By having your basic needs taken care of; food, shelter, water and love; you will have the time freedom most adventurers seek. Could you imagine money coming into your bank account for doing what you love? Could you imagine money coming into your bank account for doing nothing? Every month, money is deposited in you account, regardless of what you do, or whether you are worthy.

The cool thing is, you are worthy! You are worthy just by being you!

🦋 **Insight:**

Discovering your passion and continually taking action toward it is the key to having material wealth, happiness and winning the challenge.

Money never starts an idea; it is the idea that starts the money.
– William J. Cameron

Many say they want to be a millionaire or to be financially free. First of all, what is a millionaire?

Is being a millionaire having a net worth of a million dollars? Or, is being a millionaire mean having a million dollars in the bank? Is being a millionaire owning a house worth a million dollars? Actually, being a millionaire is really an arbitrary label, created by ego, placed on what we think is required to have all our desires fulfilled. What the ego doesn't tell you, it will never be enough. You may say you want a certain job and you will be successful. Then you get the job, and you say when I have money for "fill in the blank" I will be happy. Then you acquire "fill in the blank" and you say when I have more "fill in the blank" I will be happy. This loop keeps going on perhaps for your entire adventure. Your true mission, or destiny card gets derailed by your ego and the fog of materialism.

Being happy is not a number on your bank statement, rather it is a state of mind.

If we feel abundant- we will have more abundance.

Your reality of money is the energy you give it.

Like all things in the universe, money is energy and is powered by the energy we give it emotionally.

For example, if we are in fear of losing money – we will probably lose it.

If we feel we have to work hard and long for money- we will.

If we feel we don't have enough- we won't.

If we feel worried about the lack of it -we will lack.

If we feel happy about how much we have -we will be happy.

If we are joyful, we can share with others- we will have more to share.

If we are grateful for all we have- we will have more to be grateful for.

Lower vibrating thoughts and feelings about money will repel, while positive thoughts and feelings will attract.

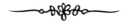

🦋 Insight:

Higher vibrating feelings of love, happiness and joy while focusing on your desires and dreams are the key to unlock your vault. Living your life in this higher vibration with focus will manifest everything you desire.

The winds of grace are always blowing. It is you that must raise your sails.
 – Rabindranath Tagore

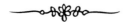

Staying in higher vibrating emotions will help you create or manifest in your material life. The action of acquiring money solely to survive this material terrain should not take precedence over discovering your gift to the world.

When asked, most people will say being financially free means having the time to do what they really want to do, rather than having to work at a job for money.

What does being financially free FEEL like for you?

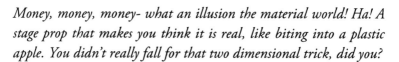 *Dear Money Bags,*

Money, money, money- what an illusion the material world! Ha! A stage prop that makes you think it is real, like biting into a plastic apple. You didn't really fall for that two dimensional trick, did you?

Your Eternal Banker,
 Infinity

 **Insight:**

Being wealthy is not about the amount of money in your bank account. It is a FEELING of abundance and a state of mind. Once you begin walking the path toward your passion, your enthusiasm will attract abundance.

When you discover your mission, you will feel its demand. It will fill you with enthusiasm and a burning desire to get to work on it.
   – W. Clement Stone

The Superhero's Rules about Money

1. You are not your stuff.

Having stuff does not make you better than any other adventurer. Most importantly, not having a lot of stuff does not make you less magnificent.

Nor, is acquiring a lot of stuff a measurement on how happy you are or whether you will win your game. In the story A Christmas Carol, by Charles Dickens, Scrooge acquired a lot of material wealth, but had forgotten the meaning and joy of life. When money or wealth comes before people and relationships, it is an indication you may be heading down the path toward a pitfall of the ego.

Conversely, we know of people who display modest material possessions, who live joyous, abundant, passion filled lives. This contradiction shows the flaw in this ego driven concept.

One of the big pitfalls in this game is chasing money to acquire material stuff to increase your self-worthiness. Impressing your friend and relatives by buying the big house or impressing acquaintances and strangers by buying the sports car, expensive jewelry, fancy clothes or expensive gifts, does not increase your likelihood of receiving abundance.

In fact the opposite is true. Doing these things to gain validation lowers your vibration, which lowers your ability to manifest.

These actions transmit the vibration you are not worthy enough just as you are.

It is important to emphasize, the action of desiring or acquiring the material objects in itself, does not lower your vibration. Your feelings of non-worthiness and inadequacy, is what lowers your vibration and contradicts your material manifestation.

The universe will seek to match your feelings and vibration of not enough, although you think your thoughts are on acquiring material objects. When your feelings are incongruent to thought; for example, you are so stressed out about bills and money, and can't get to bed at night. The Universe will not deliver your abundance.

This is where some may think the law of attraction does not work. They are thinking about and imagining their new sports car, but the feeling of wanting to impress others is a feeling of lack or current inadequacy.

2. Define your passion

All adventurers have selected a different destiny card to live out on Earth. You are unique. Your gifts, talents and natural ability are exclusively aligned to help you to accomplish living out your destiny- your ideal life. Deep within you, below the cosmic amnesia you know this. Your destiny card is calling if you feel like something is missing in your life. You are not fulfilled or happy and are going through the motion of life with no enthusiasm or joy. The closer your get to your target, the better you will feel. Like the hot cold game you played as child, your emotions will tell you when you are getting close to your passion (hot), or moving further from it (cold) by your emotional barometer. When you are getting hot, you vibrate in the higher emotions of happiness, joy, fun, and enthusiasm. You will be in the zone. You absolutely love your passion. You are full of enthusiasm when you talk or think about it. Time stands still when you are taking action. Everything goes magically well. You become reenergized.

As adventurer's we love to see our teammates (other Earth adventurers) accomplish their destiny. It is the most beautiful event to witness. We love to see athletes accomplish the previously impossible or Olympians win gold medals. We clamor to see performers or artists who exhibit their souls and touch our hearts with the beauty of the universe radiating from their gifts. They are living their dream! Destiny card accomplished!

✉ *Dear Super Hero,*

Be bold, be daring, be larger than life!
The world needs your gift today. There is no time to spare as super heros unite!

Marveling at Your Magnificence,
 Infinity

3. Define your purpose within your passion and take action toward it

Hidden within your passion is your purpose. Passion without purpose lacks the power to align the forces of the universe. Passion alone can be fulfilling; a hobby, something done well and enjoyed. Success trainers recognize the importance of identifying purpose. A great athlete without a purpose may never be discovered. The defined purpose is the driving force to endure what is necessary to accomplish destiny and bring your passion to the world. What is your big purpose? Your purpose may be to win the gold medal, to be the best in the sport, to paint a masterpiece, to help a million people, to be a teacher, to discover a cure, to the be a president of nations, to change the world. The vision of your purpose has to be bigger than the comfort of your current reality.

Discovering your destiny is like a treasure hunt, actually it is the greatest adventure of your life. You are given clues to discover your passion and it is up to you to figure out the secret code or driving purpose to unlock your destiny card. You are the only superhero capable of deciphering the clues and taking the purpose-filled action necessary. It is never too late! The world needs your destiny and you are the only one who can deliver.

Play it big! The universe needs a super hero who is playing full out. Success, fulfillment and material success are at your fingertips.

4. Have a vision - Visualize with all your senses and feel accomplishment today

Mighty adventurer! You have identified your passion and purpose- it is time to create a vision. The vision is how this passion and purpose plays out in your life. What does your life look like with your passion and purpose accomplished? Use all your senses and imagine what a typical day would feel like, what would you see and hear? Where do you live? How does money flow to you?

Why do you want success and abundance? Start window shopping and create your ideal vision. List all your desires in detail. Let your imagination soar. Once you see it in your mind, you can create your vision in reality. Review this vision often. The road will unfold to take you to your visualized destination magically.

✦ Insight:

A clear vision of a destination is critical to a successful arrival.

No man has ever been known to succeed without applying the principle of definiteness of purpose.
– Andrew Carnegie

5. The power of the written word

Writing is a powerful and magical tool. When writing you take non-tangible thoughts and make them manifest in the material world.

A college study showed that 3% of the graduating class practiced writing down their goals. A follow up twenty years later found that the 3% that had written down their goals were worth more financially than the other 97% combined! It also appeared that this 3% were more successful in other ways, too, such as having happy relationships.

Goal writing is like preparing a map for your future. The more specific your goal the more intense focus is attracted to it. It should also be written in present tense as if it is happening now. And as with all words they should be stated positively, and be something we are moving toward and not away from.

When you write something down, you activate powerful unseen forces of the universe. The simple act of writing focuses our words, desires and beliefs like a laser beam activating the universe to action. You are designing your future and inviting Synchronicity and Grace to join the party! When you write something down you are creating a menu of entrees for the universe to prepare and serve to you.

 Insight:

The magic is activated when take pen to paper and write down your goals, dreams and ideal future life.

If it is not written down, it does not exist.
    – Anais Nin

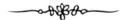

6. Gratitude and appreciation

Gratitude is another magical tool in the quiver of the superhero adventurer. Feeling and expressing gratitude magically opens the doorway for more things to be grateful for to come your way. Daily writing of things you are grateful uses the magic of the written word and grace of gratitude to super-size the potion.

So, what does this really mean?

Talking about and complaining about your current house, means you grow farther from the house of your dreams.

Solution: Be grateful for the shelter your current house offers and think of all the things you appreciate about your current home. While feeling happy and abundant, create a detailed written list of all the features in your 'perfect home'. Post it where you can see it often.

It means you get farther from the promotion by griping about how out of touch your boss is.

It means you grow farther from your financial abundance each time you complain about the bills, or how expensive gas is, or how your ex-husband never pays child support and this is why you never have any money.

Hear this! Stop!

It is critical to your abundance. Feeling grateful today about what you have is a key to unlocking the magic.

⊠ *Dear Adventurer,*

Close your eyes and feel the abundance all around you.
I have already provided all your abundance . . . you can feel it now, can't you? Have faith and know you are attracting all abundance you desire.

Your Infinite Banker,
  Infinity

7. Give

Money is energy and must keep flowing to keep velocity. Stagnant money does not attract more money. Giving is a powerful way to keep money flowing. The Universe, in infinite wisdom, has a fulfilling giving cycle. As you give and bless others you move closer toward abundance. As you awaken your destiny and share your chosen gifts with the world, material abundance is attracted to you, and continues to flow toward you. As you continue to give, you assist others in awakening their destiny and the giving cycle keeps giving toward infinity. Living in the infinite is where your magnificent spirit is returns home on earth.

 Insight:

Abundance creates more abundance.

The man who will use his skill and constructive imagination to see how much he can give for a dollar, instead of how little he can give for a dollar, is bound to succeed.
– Henry Ford

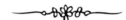

Whether or not you aspire to being a millionaire is not important. What is important is that you feel you are free, financially and otherwise, to take the time to do what you are passionate about. Your gift is something you love to do, not necessarily what pays the most.

It takes a courageous soul to break out of a comfy cocoon to create a new reality. Imagine you are the caterpillar becoming a beautiful butterfly.

 *Dear Faithful Visionary,*

Do you get it yet? It is not about where you are now – it is all about where you are going. Without a vision you are going in circles and going nowhere. What a joke Earth plays on you – a time loop!
The only way to get out of the loop is to live your vision in your mind first!

Your Eternal Optometrist,
Infinity

Material manifestation can occur when your emotions, energy flow, and intuition align.

Material manifestation or desire is not greedy. It is the energy behind the desire, which determines greed or gratitude. Super heroes come to this material terrain to experience the physical and enjoy it and have fun with it. It is not greedy to desire to have the experience of feeling what the physical world can offer.

It is the energy behind your motivation, which creates greed. Greed is a pitfall of the ego-always wanting more for the sake of just having more stuff, or to keep up with the Joneses. The opposite of greed is giving, which is why giving or tithing is so powerful. It is a very high vibration. When you give you open up to receiving more.

Your adventure is not only about acquiring a lot of stuff. Your adventure is not about denying material luxuries. Your adventure is about fulfilling your destiny and creating the life of your dreams. It is about creating your life, unlimited, expanding, and unrestricted by the material, enhanced by the material. It is about time freedom. Freedom to have the space to discover what makes your heart sing.

Chapter 8:
Having Faith, Engaging the Magic

Everything is really all right. Up until now, you did not have the rules to navigate life in this challenge successfully. Now you have the tools to Awaken your Destiny and create the life you desire. Know today, everything is working in your best interest and will work out perfectly. You feel no trepidation about your future. No worries, no fears. You know from this point forward that everything always works out for you. Believe and trust that you are blessed. You are guided by your intuition and protected by the most powerful force, the Universe. The Universe loves you.

Your emotions are your navigational system and the catalyst to integrate the creation process through intuition. Along with emotional vibration, there are personal character traits, which assist in the flow creation. Some of these have been discussed in earlier chapters, and are worth restating.

Commitment- Be committed to the experience of connecting with your intuition. There is no half way. Once you dive off the edge of the cliff, you are committed to the experience of cliff diving. There is no turning back. Commitment creates perseverance, discipline and decisiveness. It creates a fountain of inner strength, which will help you persevere in situations, which may deter others.

Words and Thoughts – Your words and thoughts are powerful energy. Practice the use of empowering words and thoughts. Further, do no harm to others in thought, word and deed. Understand there is an interconnection to everything and we all have an integral part to play in the grand scheme of life.

Honesty- Operating in honesty, we commit to honor the truth. Integrity focuses our energy toward empowerment. Do what you say you are going to do. Live your life with honor. We may need to integrate parts of ourselves as we delve deeper into our intuitive connection, This requires being brutally honest with ourselves to identify and break through layers of self- deceptions, emotional scars, limiting and self sabotaging beliefs, internal conflicts and releasing of buried hopes, dreams and fears. Be honest with yourself and in the moment each challenge arises, choose in the direction of honor and integrity.

Courage-Have the courage to step out of our current comfort zones, and follow intuitive hunches. Courageous is the soul whom commits to the larger plan of Awakening Destiny.

Passion- Find the passion for life, for discovery, in everything you do. Passion and enthusiasm are high range, high vibration emotions which bring you closer to your intuitive connection. Live your life with passion.

Living in the Now- The present moment is the only point of power in which you can connect to your intuition. Don't waste it fretting about the past or worrying about the future.

Receiving- Listen to your inner voice and receive all gifts. By graciously receiving we are in harmony with the moment and connection. Be open – know all things are possible.

Positivity- Use positive words, thoughts and beliefs. Know every situation holds a gift. Be positive and know all things will always work out just as it is intended.

Trust- Having a good feeling toward action, some people will call it a hunch. Following an intuitive hunch and trusting your intuition is an important step in your connection to your higher self.

Faith- Having Faith is the key to pulling your beautiful creation called your life together. Faith is the deep calm that resides deep in the core of your being that knows all is well.

Some may confuse faith with religion. Religion is the practice created by man to worship the Divine. There are many religions and religious practices. For some, basking in their religious practice elevates their energy of connectedness to God, in which case religion and faith become intertwined. For some, faith can exist without religion. For some, connectedness with God can exist without religion.

Having faith and engaging in the magic of life is available to everyone. Every adventurer from every creed, color and religion is a superhero waiting to be discovered!

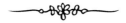

 Insight:

Everything we require to manifest our highest destiny is already here within our reach.

If you follow your bliss, you put yourself on a kind of track that has been there all the while, waiting for you, and the life that you ought to be living.
– Joseph Campbell

Every change in your life is a glorious adventure, and because you have faith it will, all things work out for you. Go with change and focus on the positive perception. Have faith change is good. Change allows us to grow, experience new people, places and things. Change creates a space in which intuition can speak to you, and act through you. Embracing change will bring more positive energy into your life, simply because you expect it and believe it.

📧 *Dear Stargazer,*

Your destiny is today!
You are living your destiny NOW. Surprise!
You are more beautiful than all the constellations in the sky,

Your Ultimate Astronomer,
  Infinity

Each day you are creating the life you are living, until now perhaps unconsciously. Now you are aware of your emotional navigational system and know how to keep your energetic vibrational frequency high. Each day, going forward as you are consciously creating, you are on your path and living and awakening your destiny one step at a time. You are on your perfect path to awakening destiny! Take a step on the path of your destiny each day. How do you know if you are on the right path? Trust in your navigational system! Is it fun? Does it raise your energy vibration by bringing joy, laughter and happiness? If yes, you are on the right path. Destiny is the place you are living daily, you may not know what the final out come is now, and all you may see is the next step. Take inspired action in the direction that feels good.

Think about what things you enjoy doing right now. Don't try to figure out how you can make money or a career out of what brings you enthusiastic enjoyment. Just have fun doing all the activities you enjoy and that make you feel good.

You can have many passions in your life and do them all simultaneously.

Think about someone who inspires you who is on a path you admire. Is this what you want for yourself? If so, imagine how this person feels and what they would do if they were where you are today, and take action. Keep the inspiration and let it flow, as more than one person may inspire you. Blend these inspirations and take action. This creates your unique you.

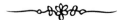

 Insight:

Follow your heart and go with what brings enthusiasm and enjoyment in your life and be in the flow- this will lead you to another fun place.

You don't have to see the whole staircase, just the next step.
 – Martin Luther King, Jr.

Play it BIG! Expand your comfort zone, take steps toward your vision and close the gap between your life now and the life you are creating. Accept change and the challenges of expansion with the enthusiasm of the great adventurer you are. Greeting change with hope, enthusiasm, flexibility and a positive outlook will transform your life.

Be what you want to become.

If you want abundance, be abundance. Feel, think and act, like someone who is abundant.

If you want peace, be peace. Feel, think and act, like someone who is peaceful.

If you want health, be health. Feel, think and act, like someone who is healthful.

 Insight:

Do what you love. Do what inspires you and fills you up. Do what is fun. Follow your bliss. This is the road leading you toward your destiny.

Believe in yourself, and the world will believe in you!.
 – Jim Oleson

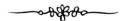

Allowing inspiration is giving up the egos version of how your life is supposed to be. Letting go of what the neighbors will think and what others will say about you. Only you know your true destiny and only you can make this journey toward your heart. This could mean being willing to give up earthly security. It could mean doing something new, crazy and fun. It could mean moving half way around the world. It could mean volunteering at a local non-profit. It could mean nurturing the soul of your child.

✉ *Dear Twinkle Toes,*

Life is like a dance; sometimes it is fast like the quick step, sometimes slow like the waltz. You can never predict what music life will be playing. Some days will feel cosmically better than others. Regardless of the tempo of the day, whatever you do, don't stop dancing and above all have fun!

In Breathless Adoration,
   Infinity

The Universe has a great plan for you. The Universe knows how everything plays out, and is always watching out for you. We cannot see with our linear eyes, the broad horizon and greatness the universe has in store for us. Step toward faith and the multi dimensional world opens up before our eyes. Your future is no longer a random chain of events. You are now navigating and creating your future.

A Place of Quiet Bliss

Each day spend time in aloneness, basking in the communion with infinity. Be in silence by yourself. Turn off the radio in the car and be with your self. Wake up and greet the dawn in quiet meditation. Kiss the sunset goodnight in silent revelry. Focus on the quiet and let the universe fill in the notes. It is in the silence we hear the quiet whisper of our spirit.

Allow inspiration. Create the beautiful music of your life.

 Dear Maestro,

Take good care to listen in the silence between the notes, as this is where the symphony of your soul takes place.

In the Melody of Bliss,
    Infinity

You Have Arrived!

Here's a secret.

Your destiny is not a singular destination. Your destiny is not a place somewhere out there, in a far away place to be discovered many years from now. It is not a place you will arrive many tomorrows from now and say, "I finally made it." Your destiny is today. Your destiny is an intertwined matrix of events that occur in your life every day. Make a difference today. Believe each day you live, carves your destiny. Believe each person you meet, carves your destiny. Live your life in glorious splendor. Look for the miracle each day brings. Light speed on your journey; the journey of the courageous! You are the luckiest adventurer you know!

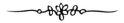

 Insight:

Our deepest fear is not that we are inadequate
Our deepest fear is that we are powerful beyond measure
It's our light, not our darkness that most frightens us
We ask ourselves, Who am I to be brilliant, gorgeous, talented and fabulous?
Actually, who are you not to be?
You are a child of God.

Your playing small does not serve the world.
There is nothing enlightened about shrinking so other people won't feel
insecure around you.
We were born to make manifest the glory of God that is within us.
It is not just in some of us, it is in everyone.
And as we let our own light shine, we unconsciously give permission
to other people to do the same.
As we are liberated from our own fear, our presence automatically
liberates others.

    – Nelson Mandela

CPSIA information can be obtained at www.ICGtesting.com
Printed in the USA
BVOW071046110412

287350BV00003B/1/P